The Post in the Hills

Other books by Katharine Stewart include:

A Croft in the Hills
Crofts and Crofting
A Garden in the Hills
A School in the Hills

The Post
in the Hills

KATHARINE STEWART

THE MERCAT PRESS
EDINBURGH

First published in 1997 by Mercat Press
at James Thin, 53 South Bridge
Edinburgh EH1 1YS

ISBN: 1873644 744

Set in Bauer Bodoni and Garamond at Mercat Press
Printed and bound in Great Britain by
Redwood Books, Trowbridge, Wiltshire

To celebrate the work of all those bearers of great tidings—
from the runners of old to the Post Bus drivers of today

Contents

Illustrations

Foreword

For over thirty-five years now we have been involved, as a family, with one of the smallest Post Offices in the Highlands. Small and down-to-earth as it is, it has forged for me a strong sense of linkage with the early days of the postal service. Times of snow and storm have meant delivery of mail on foot, as in the days of the 'runners'. With the breakdown of telephone communications urgent messages have been taken round by word of mouth.

The office is the natural centre for the dissemination of news affecting the area, where the activities of the Community Council, of the School Board, of the Village Hall Committee can all be scrutinised and discussed, as in former times the newspapers would be perused, the Postmaster charging a small fee for reading them aloud!

There is a linkage with the future, too, now that computerisation has reached even the smallest outposts. But that is another story. The past, the present and the future of the postal service, this great effort in communication, all hold fast to the watchword of service. We've come a long way since the first recorded 'runner', bringing news of victory in battle, died after accomplishing his mission. But I reckon he considered himself privileged to have been given the task, as, in a small way, we feel a certain sense of privilege in being, by stamping and dating and processing the mail, the bearers of news to people in many parts of the world.

From the bushman putting his ear to the ground to the advent of the silicon chip, between the foot-post and the sender of electronic mail there is a vast gap in the story of communication. The bridging of this gap has been accomplished by the ingenuity and energy of many people. Science has performed miracles beyond the reach of the imagination. But in our small corner we have been able to keep in close touch with the human side of things, the look in the eye, the touch of the hand, as news, good or bad, is communicated. In the record of day-to-day doings in the story of the postal service we can almost feel the weariness in the bones of the 'runners', hear the hoof-beats of the Surveyor's horse, the sound of the mail-coach horn. Here, in the Highlands, we can still follow the foot-post's track, the coaching inns where the horses were changed are still there, as are the little toll-houses, where the gates were flung wide for the passage of the mail-coach. 'Acceleration' is a key word in most facets of life today. But I'm glad to have been involved in the service of the Post Office when speed was not necessarily of the essence, when time still seemed as limitless as space and there was enough to spare for the exchange of greetings, for a blessing here, a good wish there, a sharing of whatever the day held, as the simple routine of work went on.

I should like to thank many people for help in the preparation of this book—Mr Steward and his staff at Highland Archives, where a box of old letters set me on a trail, Miss Mackenzie at Inverness Museum who dug out old photographs, Dr James Mackay, whose handbook on the postal history of the Islands and other publications provide an invaluable source of information, Mr and Mrs J.A. Mackintosh who lent me many of these books, Mr Martin Cummins and Mr Alistair Ramsay of the Scottish Post Office Board in Edinburgh and Mr Adam Borwick of the Royal Mail (Scotland and Northern Ireland) for generous help with illustrations and encouragement, the staffs of Royal Mail and Post Office Counters, Inverness, and of the Post Office Archives in London and, of course, Tom Johnstone of the Mercat Press for his ever-ready guidance.

I

Letters from the Highlands

When we inherited the charge of running the small Post Office, along with the tenancy of the old schoolhouse, in the hills above Loch Ness, some 35 years ago, we had little inkling of how the systems of communication had evolved over the centuries, or, indeed, how they were to develop during the ensuing decades.

To us, as to many people, the Post Office was, in our early years, the place where you could buy stamps and postal orders, cash orders, make deposits in a Savings Bank, post a parcel, send a telegram. Everything was weighed and calculated, often from behind slightly intimidating metal bars, by slightly intimidating, often elderly, personnel. Letters were delivered by postmen who were most often unseen when they came in the early hours and pushed the envelopes through a slit in the front door. We remembered the arrival of the telegram boy, wearing his little round, chin-strapped hat, who handed in his little yellow envelope and waited to see if a reply was needed. He was greeted with trepidation, followed most often, mercifully, by relief.

We had collected stamps, of course, in our young days, and postcards, but it had never really occurred to us to wonder how the perilous journey of a fragile piece of paper from, say, one of the more remote small islands of the Hebrides to our doorstep was accomplished successfully for our delight. Now, with a book of stamps to hand, scales, weights, a date-stamp, forms of all kinds, we began to think about how the whole business of communication world-wide was managed.

For a start, we looked back to our first days in the hill land where we had come to live and work. Our post arrived in early afternoon. We saw its bearer from a distance as he came down through a patch of felled woodland from the road where he had left his motor-bike. He was one of our nearest neighbours—Bill-the-Post—

and his coming was always welcomed with a blether, an exchange of news, sometimes a cup of tea, even when his delivery consisted of small buff envelopes containing bills or forms. On days of storm he would battle his way through waist-high drifts of snow to deliver the mail. Many times, when his round was done and his own well-tended croft was not demanding attention, he would give us a hand at whatever job we were at—getting a crop in before the weather broke, seeing to a sick cow or finishing some fencing to keep the roe out of the turnips.

In older times, before the luxury of a delivery to the door had been introduced, a letter would have to be collected from the nearest receiving office, probably the one in Inverness, ten miles away. Here, the postmaster would stand in the market place on market day, and call out the names of any persons from the country for whom letters had arrived, perhaps from relatives who had emigrated to the towns in the south or to countries overseas.

From the late 1700s, when a school had been established here by the Scottish Society for the Propagation of Christian Knowledge, it is probable that the schoolmaster would have kept for collection letters sent by a 'runner' from the town. He would have also seen to the despatch of mail by the same means. And he would, on request, have read the letters to recipients who had never attended school and also write answers at their bidding. In some places, letter-writers earned a small fee performing this task. Even in our day, fingers roughened by years of toil took badly to the handling of pen on paper.

With all the facilities we have for the writing of letters today it's sad that so few are written. Telephonic messages are essentially ephemeral. There is poetry in speaking to a beloved in a far-off place while walking in the garden, an instrument tucked close to ear and mouth. But where is the relic, to be read over, thought about, cherished and put away for future reference? Luckily, in the Highlands, we have had letter-writers of great talent who have left us priceless records of the times they wrote in. Mrs Grant of Laggan, wife of the local minister, wrote letters to many friends, over a period of years, which were eventually published in London in 1809, in three volumes, entitled *Letters from the Mountains, being the real correspondence of a lady between the years 1773 and 1807*. She travelled quite extensively round the country and in her letters discusses many topics, social and political, as well as personal and domestic matters, illness, bereavement and so on. A picture of the times certainly emerges. The publication was well received and went into four editions.

Captain Burt, an officer of engineers, was sent into Scotland about 1730 as a 'contractor'. After his return he published, in 1754, his *Letters from a Gentleman in the North of Scotland to his Friend in London*. There was a strict injunction that they were to be shown to no one but one nameless friend, but this was clearly disregarded when they appeared in book form. One can understand his fear of possible lynching when reading his description of a 'Capital Town in that Northern Country'—obviously Inverness. He talks of the squalor of the 'Huts' and streets, the filth of the inhabitants and their strange ways. Fortunately for him these hapless people had no contact with him or his writings. There must have been many places furth of the border where similar conditions prevailed. His descriptions of other parts of the country, where his engineering skills would have given him a different outlook, are, however, valuable. He talks of roads, bridges, ferries and so on. There is a definite impression that he has an eye on methods of 'civilising' the ignorant peasantry. Could he have been a Government spy?

Our great writers, too, have found time to send letters to fellow-writers which give us fascinating insights into the world of literature and of literary criticism and also glimpses of the personal lives of the writers. Fortunately many of these letters have been preserved in book form. The original copies are in the National Library in Edinburgh. Neil Gunn, Naomi Mitchison, Hugh MacDiarmid have left us letters which show how their minds worked, what influences they accepted and bestowed, how they reacted to criticism, what were their relations with the world at large. Their problems in matters of finance, ill-health and domestic arrangements are also touched on, giving us a rounded picture of the human being pushing the pen.

Today the air-waves must be resounding with like messages, but where are they? Lost among the clouds or stars? Perhaps recorded in the minds of recipients, but ephemeral as life itself.

The writing of diaries or journals, not meant originally for publication, has also been largely abandoned. The one I keep myself I find invaluable, not for the re-reading of any profound reflections inscribed therein, but as an *aide-mémoire*, reminding me of when certain things took place—a meeting, a visit to friends, the posting of an important letter.

Dorothy Wordsworth's *Journal* of a tour she and her famous brother made of parts of the Highlands gives us glimpses of the conditions of the time, descriptions of the houses, of the inns, of the food provided. William's poem about the 'solitary Highland lass' does show some empathy with the people.

Queen Victoria was an indefatigable diary writer and no mean artist. Her sketches of Highland people and places are full of life. She writes mainly, of course, about the daily doings of herself and her entourage, but she also describes meetings with the real people of the country. She went to watch the sheep-dipping, which she called 'juicing the sheep' and 'salmon leistering', catching the salmon driven into nets or speared, attended the Games and a christening and visited many elderly women, of whom she became really fond. Between these entries there are references to events in the outside world such as the death of the Duke of Wellington, the fall of Sevastopol. The *Leaves from the Journal of our Life in the Highlands 1848-1861* was published in London in 1868; *More Leaves 1862-82* was published in 1884.

The Memoirs of a Highland Lady, the Autobiography of Elizabeth Grant of Rothiemurchus 1797-1830 is another delightful book, recording the daily life of a family of the minor Highland aristocracy. There are accounts of hardship and happiness, rising at six on winter mornings and breaking the ice in the jug to wash, picnics in the hills, boating on the river, dancing and singing. The outside world is always there, in the background. When Napoleon threatens to invade the south there is talk of raising a body of hardy volunteers from among the local people. Is anyone today, I wonder, recording life in this charming and authentic way, so that future generations can appreciate the truth of the past?

II
Early Days

As time went by old houses were being renovated and more telephones installed. There were more cars around. People could commute to town for work, post letters and buy stamps there. But did they, we wondered, have time to write letters anyway? Telephone communication was fast and to the point, but what was it doing to the language? Was everything to be abbreviated, reduced to the monosyllable or to capital letters? Already, in our relations with what we then called the 'Head Office' in town and which have always been most cordial and helpful, we were having to get used to referring to official forms by acronyms. Sometimes, in confusion, when consulting on the phone, we would have to invent an urgent customer at the door so as hurriedly to look up the real name of the form referred to.

Letter-writing was not really dead. At Christmas, from friends in far-off places, letters would come recounting the events of a whole year in their lives. These were welcome, though they lacked the intimacy of a personal letter, for we knew that they went out to a host of other people who were strangers to us. Only a short note at the end and the signature were really directed at ourselves. What joy it was to find, among the drab little scraps of official paper, an envelope addressed by a known hand and inside at least two whole pages in the same hand, detailing events and thoughts expressly for our delight!

Letter-writing has been an important form of communication since the earliest times. Writing itself originated as far back as 3,000 B.C. in the country we now call Iraq, which has been known as the cradle of civilisation. It was pictographic, that is, consisted of pictures of familiar objects used as signs. This developed into cuneiform (wedge-shaped) writing, which reduced the pictures to simpler signs, representing syllables. Gradually the number of signs was reduced

A cuneiform letter from Ur, written between 2100 and 2000 B.C.

to about 300. The early scripts soon spread from Babylon to neighbouring peoples and then to the Greeks, the Etruscans and the Romans, who later developed their own styles. In the sixth century A.D. a form of writing known as Ogham had spread to Scotland from southern Ireland. It is based on a form of 'finger' language, with strokes in a series of five, and is found on the stone monuments erected by the Picts.

How did they write? About 2,000 years B.C. the Assyrians and the Egyptians were composing messages inscribed on tablets of baked clay. Messenger services, of course, have been in existence since the earliest times, when the strongest and fastest young runners would be chosen for the task. There is the famous story of the runner from Marathon, in 490 B.C., who fell dead on arrival with the news of victory. When writing was discovered runners would carry a message written on their shaven skulls. Their hair grew on the journey and on arrival at their destination their heads were shaved again to reveal the message.

The Pharaohs had a system of express messengers who delivered the tablets travelling on small punts in the network of canals in the valley of the Nile. About 500 years B.C. the Persian king, as Herodotus relates, set up a relay service of mounted messengers. There was also a service across the desert, linking the oases.

The Greeks had a courier system, messages being written on the skins of animals. News was also sent from island to island by means of lighted torches. The Romans developed a sophisticated, well-regulated postal service with relays of mounted couriers and light, two-wheeled vehicles drawn by two horses, which could cover distances easily over the network of well-maintained roads. The first mail-coaches! They wrote on wax tablets with a stylus.

In the Bible (*Esther* chapters 3, 4, and 8) we hear of 'the king's scribes' writing letters, sealed with the king's seal, to be sent to the provincial governors and of letters 'sent by posts on horseback' and riders on 'mules, camels and young dromedaries.' In the New Testament we read that Paul's first epistle to the Romans was 'written to the Romans from Corinthus and sent by Phebe, servant of the church at Cenchrea.'

As time went by developments progressed. The Egyptians began to use papyrus, a rush grown in the delta of the Nile, as writing material. Gradually, about the sixth century A.D., it was superseded by parchment, which was made from calf skin or the tanned hides of sheep or goats. Eventually, paper, made from cotton fibres, came from China. Later, it was made from rags and wood pulp and it is still the main material used for writing, to the detriment of many valuable forests. In India palm leaves, tied with pieces of kelp, were used for writing up to the ninetheenth century and were accepted by the British postal authorities. Sharpened reeds were used for writing on paper. Then a bird's feather, known now as a quill, was found to be effective. The word pen comes from the Latin for a feather and the French word *plume* means both feather and pen.

I have in my possession a goose quill and a bottle of 'ink', made by soaking a rusty nail in water, both of which were in use last century by a man from the hills. Until the nineteenth century letters were folded and sealed with wax. My grandfather wore a wide gold 'signet' ring, with his initials emblazoned on it, which he used for sealing his letters, even after the introduction of envelopes. I well remember the delicious smell of hot sealing wax! And I remember my grandmother receiving 'crossed' letters, letters written both down and across the page. This was to save paper and to save weight in the post and so to save the cost of postage. Some were difficult to decipher!

As time went by we heard of the different places in the area still known as the 'Old Post Office', where postal business had been done. One house is a rickle of stones now, but others have been maintained and modernised. In the days when Loch Ness was an important thoroughfare through the great glen, the postie would go down to the pier to collect the mails, take them to the 'office' (his kitchen) to be sorted, then set out to deliver them. A bicycle was provided, but many places could only be reached on foot, and on days of winter snow and storm his hours of duty extended well into the night. Many of these far-away places are now, sadly, uninhabited.

In our early days Bill-the-Post still followed this procedure, taking the out-going mail, not to the steamer but to the bus, and collecting the in-coming for sorting. His motor-bike he ran at his own expense, being allowed only a pedal cycle by the authorities. Often in winter no other form of transport was of any help, with frost and snow lying on the steep hill road, which rises to 800 feet in a mile and a half. Many times, in spring, summer, autumn and winter, it must have been irksome to have his day taken up with the post, when his crops and beasts were needing attention. But his sense of duty was strict and he never failed to deliver.

He took a spell of leave, at appropriate times, of course, usually coinciding with an important time in the crofting year, sowing or harvest. Then a temporary substitute would do the round. There was always someone local ready to do the job. There was a time when what were known as 'soap coupons'—the junk mail of the day—were bulking up the mail-bag. One substitute postie, fretting at having to carry these scraps of paper, which would be discarded as soon as delivered, to the high and outlying places, stuffed a bundle of them into a whin-bush. That night a gale blew up and the coupons were scattered far and wide. Some were gathered up by excited children, hoping for a reward, some were used to kindle fires.

Our postie, being a native of the place, was known to every household. At that time there were few incomers. He could keep his peers acquainted with the ongoings of the neighbourhood—the home-comings, the departures, illness or death. His arrival was a high-point of the day. Even the soap coupons, the vet's bill, or the latest form from the Department of Agriculture, commonly known as the 'Board', any or all of these were accepted gladly when they brought the chance of a 'news' with the post.

Collecting the post from a roadside letter-box near Callander
(The Post Office)

Some people may have envied him his job, for it did provide him with a small but steady income. Others pitied him for having to devote so much time to it when he might have been tending a sick ewe or rushing the hay in before a sudden summer storm. When his retiral day came we met in the schoolhouse for a ceilidh. By removing all the furniture except the chairs and a small table we managed to squeeze a good crowd into the sitting-room. An official came out from the town to make the presentation of a gold watch. Bill, a little reluctantly, made a short but happy speech. We had Gaelic songs, stories in the old style and many a goodnight dram.

Thereafter things were organised differently. The mail came out, ready sorted, in a smart red van, driven by a postman from the town. We were to be only part of a wider round. Was there an increase in efficiency? I doubt it. There was certainly a decrease in the involvement of the postmaster with the mail. It arrived in neat bundles, packed away in the van. 'Himself' handled only the official communications and his own personal letters. There was no more puzzling over and re-writing of scarcely legible addresses, sometimes with the Gaelic spelling. Those letters would have to take their chance or be 'returned to sender'. We were lucky enough to have an official 'town' postman who was really a countryman by nature and even had his own small croft not far away. He made his official tea-break at Bill-the-Post's house, so keeping contact going between the old ways and the new.

After his retirement Bill was able to devote all his time to the work of his croft. The older sister who had kept house for him had died long since, the two young men who had 'boarded' with them had been sent to other places. He had everything to do, but still his place was a model of good agricultural practice. One day, eager to get going with the ploughing when the weather was ideal, he went out early to start up the tractor, an old tractor with the starting handle at the front, forgetting that he had left it in gear. It darted forward, knocking him to the ground, where he lay in agony till a neighbour spotted him some time later. Shock and some cracked bones and bruises didn't keep him laid up for long.

When at last he was compelled to take things more easily I would visit him on a Sunday afternoon, giving him a hand to formulate his right to cut peats on the hill which was about to be planted with conifers. He won that one! Then he was anxious to make sure of his boundary by the loch. He was a fighter to the end. After a talk he always insisted on making tea and providing cakes. Happily he did not have long to suffer in hospital and friends and neighbours thronged his bedside over his last days. His place is safely in the hands of a relative now and a neighbour's cattle graze the fields. When, in his turn, Bill's successor, Kenny Chisholm, reached retiring age we wondered who our next postie would be.

John Kay had acted as substitute on several occasions and he now stepped into the breach quite happily. He was familiar with the round, had coped with it in all weathers, knew the exact spot on the hill where the wheels would start spinning in the frost, the boggy bits to avoid on the way to the isolated crofts. He had covered rounds in various places in his day and was very much a countryman, with a special love of gardening. Many times we discussed plants, their likes and dislikes. In summer he never passed the border without stopping to admire a bloom and to breathe in its scent. He entered into all our enthusiasms and many times he brought small things he had come across on his journeys to add to the museum collection. His family had had connections with the postal service for over 200 years. He has in his possession a whistle which a forebear would blow to summon people to collect their letters at the Receiving Office.

However, he was not to be our new permanent 'man of letters'. This was to be Willy Urquhart, who also knew the round well and was also a born countryman. As I write he is still faithfully working his round, doing many acts of kindness and always with unfailing cheerfulness. A smile and a joke will always carry the day. He brightens many a community ceilidh and has displayed a hidden talent as a raconteur.

III
Shared News

We soon came to realise that running the Post Office was something more than having a 'job'. We were on a modest pay-roll, we had hours of work—9 to 1 in the morning, 4 to 5.30 in the late afternoon. We had records to keep, forms to fill in, stamps to sell, queries to answer, but we also had human beings to deal with. The three hours of freedom in the afternoon were invaluable for working in the garden or doing repair jobs on the house. But crofting people are not used to keeping set hours, so if someone turned up in mid-afternoon to cash a postal order or send off a parcel we would attend to them quite willingly. We would also attend to other needs they might have—an ear to listen to an item of good news or bad. We had a bell fixed to an outside wall in case the phone rang when we were pruning the blackcurrants. For a caller there would be a seat at the fire in winter or on a bench in the garden in summer and a cup of tea and a scone. Perhaps a son or daughter had just graduated from University. This was news that had to be shared, rejoiced in, though it was divulged shyly, so as not to appear a boast. We remembered how it always was—you never praised a child, for this was tempting providence to diminish the gifts bestowed. In very old times it was thought that the fairies might steal a sturdy baby. In actual fact it might well have been taken to build up the strength of a rival tribe.

So news of family achievement was kept in a low key, but news of loss or bereavement was something to be warmly shared. The idea of mortality was ever present in the minds of the older members of the community. When a death occurred the intimation spread over a wide area amazingly quickly. With few telephones and a reluctance on the part of most people to put pen to paper the news travelled speedily by word of mouth. This 'bush telegraph' worked almost as well as the telephonic methods of today. Sometimes the postie was asked to carry word to the more outlying places if he had mail to deliver.

Funerals were, and still are, occasions of great significance. It is important to be buried close to one's forebears and to be interred with dignity and respect, close relatives and friends helping to lower the coffin into the earth. I think this feeling dates back to the days when ancestors were 'worshipped', or at least highly regarded as the progenitors of the race. So dark clothes were taken out of cupboards for an airing. Food was prepared for those coming from a distance. Greetings and reminiscences were exchanged as people began to wend their way from the graveyard. Then it was quite in order to eat and drink, for life must go on.

These gatherings, along with those connected with work on the crofts—sheep-shearing, peat-cutting and so on—were valuable means of keeping people together in a shared acceptance of the facts of living and dying.

Most of our Post Office 'customers' had known us in our crofting days and were happy to have a 'news', knowing that we would appreciate the birth of a heifer calf or the loss of lambs in a sudden spring storm, the depredations of roe deer into the root crops or the need for repairs to the road. These exchanges over a cup of tea or a dram at New Year brought back all the feel of the time before we went into the worlds of teaching and 'posting'. As in our crofting years we had become deeply interested in the history of land use and tenure over the ages, so now we were drawn to look into the history of the 'post'.

Here we were, selling a stamp for one neighbour to send a letter to a relative ten miles away, to another to send one four hundred miles, at the same price. The postman might be delivering a packet from a town on the other side of the world to a small croft in the remote uplands. Looked at dispassionately these things do seem to have a touch of the miraculous. Not as miraculous, perhaps, as African drum-beats or the Kalahari Bushman with his ear to the ground. But—how had they come about?

We had vague recollections, from stamp-collecting days, of the 'Penny Post', of someone called Rowland Hill, of mail-coaches and 'Wells Fargo', of highwaymen and Auden's marvellous poem about the Night Mail. It all began to take shape. How had it started?

The beginnings of the service in our area we had heard about from the recollections of the neighbours. The very earliest forms of communication we had learnt about in our reading. When we had more time, we promised ourselves, we would delve into records and find out how this service, which had become indispensible world-wide, had grown and developed over the centuries.

IV
Small Post Offices

Meanwhile I was teaching in Inverness, sharing the Post Office duty at holiday-time. We had the garden to see to and I was also involved in a project undertaken by my school which meant helping in, among other things, setting up and looking after a small museum near the house. Our time was very fully, and happily, occupied. Helen, our daughter, did a stint, one year, as extra-postie, helping to deliver the Christmas mail. There was a good covering of snow at the time, so the going was hard, but it cleared the lungs of the student from Auld Reekie. The family involvement continued when, one winter, Jim had an accident, slipping on the ice and crashing into a stone wall, which landed him in hospital for several days. And I was laid up with a stomach bug! Helen, on holiday from the University, stepped quite naturally into the Postmaster's tackety boots, dealing cheerfully with customers and responding to messages of sympathy.

Days off were looked forward to and planned for weeks ahead. The occasional Monday 'public holiday', which coincided with a school long weekend, in summer, meant that we could get away sharp mid-day Saturday and be back late Monday evening. We would pack the van with camping gear, as we had always done, and make, as we had always done, for the west...

There, for close on 48 hours, we would be back in the world of the working crofts, with the scent of new-cut hay and wild flowers in June, the corn in the stook and peats in the stack if it was September, glossy black cattle on the machair, everywhere a feel of positive fruition. We'd set up camp in the dunes and wash the ink-stains from our fingers and our minds in the clear green water. The hill birds of home are fine—the buzzard with its high-planing reach and the curlew's sweet, sad call. But the white sailing of gulls over the depths of blue carries the human spirit into unknown spaces.

Melvich, a little post office in the far north of the Highlands
(The Post Office)

The taking of a longer spell of leave involved quite complicated arrangements. Whoever did the post office had to have access to the house, to understand its workings, to cope with a possible failure of the water supply, to keep the mice at bay, to remember to shut the garden gate against marauding sheep and the occasional roe-deer. There were also the many questions from passing walkers or motorists to be answered, questions about fishing rights on the loch, camp sites, rights of way, houses for sale, homes of long-lost forebears, where to get milk or drinking-water or a cup of tea, bed-and-breakfast places or even the way to an almost illegible address on a crumpled scrap of paper. There would be bona fide 'travelling people' to be welcomed and salesmen in smart cars to be sent away empty-handed.

My sister-in-law solved our problem for us. She was active and competent, having coped with several jobs during her life and now retired. She came up with a friend, took instructions from her brother, became quickly confident and ended up thoroughly enjoying her spell as sub-postmistress. The Head Office was used to dealing with situations like this and the customers treated her with their normal Highland courtesy.

So we were able to set off on longer travels—once through France to Venice where we saw Helen off to work in a kibbutz in Israel. But nothing could quite compare with our spells in the west—Morar, Arisaig, Oldshoremore (where we got milk from John Gunn whose cow was a direct descendent of the one they brought on eviction from Kildonan)—the names are like a litany.

We visited many small Post Offices in the course of our journeys, noting with interest how they managed things. Some were housed in very unsubstantial premises, small buildings with walls of corrugated iron, small sheds at some distance from a dwelling. Security, when they were established, was not the problem it has become. Then, it was still a time for the house door to be left unlocked, in case a stranger needed shelter. There was little to steal, even in a small *Oifis a'Phuist*.

We had been in our own small office for a few years, had become accustomed to regular visits from the 'Accounts' to check our balance, to supervision from a most friendly 'Surveyor' who left us a set of impeccably hand-written instructions on procedure and who entertained us, when his work was done, on a one-stringed fiddle, when news reached us that there were to be discussions about the closure of small Post Offices. Ours was certainly small. In fact, it had acquired the tag of being the smallest one in Scotland.

We began to look at it with new eyes. There it was—the stone-floored porch, a table to hold the scales and weights, the leaflets, a drawer for odds and ends, a chair for a tired customer—that was about it. But—it was also a way into a house where further welcome was assured. It was also a focal point for the area, since there was no longer a school, no church, no shop. We carried on as usual, ignoring the rumours.

V
The Post in All Weathers

That small Post Offices were to be closed was rumoured several times over the years after that. But always second thoughts prevailed. One reason, we were told, for the maintenance of the office in Abriachan was the fact of our comparative inaccessibility, which could prevent people getting to other offices five miles away on the low ground by Loch Ness. Nowadays, with tractors, Land Rovers, cars with four-wheel drive, it takes an exceptional storm to cut us off completely.

We have had them, of course. One winter the sheer volume and weight of snow on the trees, power and telephone lines was so great that the whole landscape was transformed. The birches flanking the road that rises steeply from the loch shore were bowed down on either side, completely blocking the way. Even our intrepid postie had to leave his vehicle at the foot of the hill and walk up through the drifts with his heavy bag. A neighbour and I then divided the mail between us and delivered it by hand, like the 'runners' of old, to the places we could reach, while he went to the outlying houses. Luckily there were no obviously urgent missives for the furthest away places. Those we could contact by other means were asked to collect their mail at the office, as was the custom in former times, before delivery was guaranteed.

This particular storm lasted for days. Soon telephone lines were down and the power failed. Modern households with their stand-by portable gas lamps and solid fuel cookers suffer little at such times. We were all confident that help would be forthcoming should a real emergency occur. Strong arms could clear a way for stretcher-bearers or a landing-space for the hospital helicopter. We ourselves had few devices to sustain us. We had kept to our crofting ways! But we had plenty of logs for the fire, a camping spirit stove for a quick cup of tea, coffee or soup and candles. How the 'hydro-men' manage to restore the power in the driving snow and bitter frost is beyond belief. One evening a group of them came to the door to see if we were alright.

'We saw your candle in the window.'

'Yes. Thanks. We're fine. Come in.'

Leaving their cumbersome outer gear in the porch, they approached the fire, stretching their hands to the welcoming glow. In the light from the row of candles on the mantelpiece we could see the strain on their faces. It eased as they drank cups of steaming tea, before setting off again on their all-night task.

We found a certain satisfaction in being cut off from the world, our only callers these hydro-men, who, in their strange garb, seemed almost like visitors from outer space. We had no livestock to be fed and cared for. Our cat was lying snug on the hearthrug. Everything outside was stilled, becalmed, in its great mantle of snow. The beauty of the sculpted drifts and the brilliance of the icicles was indescribable. Inside, we had books to hand and music on the radio. We could even write some letters! At night the stars were huge. It was a time apart.

We thought, of course, of neighbours who had sheep buried in the drifts. Digging them out and getting hay to them would be a task for heroes. We remembered, too, the days of the 'runners' and the mail-coaches stuck in the snow and the drivers and guards risking their lives to get the mail delivered.

We changed the date-stamp every morning, signed the daily despatch form, cleared a path from the gate and waited to see how each day would develop. During the fair, windless daylight hours the telephone men got busy and soon the bell was ringing and our isolation was over. Most places were connected to the line. It was good to be able to let people know if letters had arrived for them. We only hoped nothing urgent would come for the really far-away places which didn't have the phone.

Soon the blessed silence of the snowbound world was broken by the sound of amateur snow-plough drivers urging their machines through the drifts on the side-roads. Tractors did a useful job but diggers were apt to go too deep and lift quite a lot of the underlying surface. The official snow-plough was busy clearing the main routes down below. Our hill-road had to wait. I remembered an old neighbour of ours who had knocked up a snow-plough, just a triangular concoction of wood, which he pulled with his horse. This worked successfully when the snow was soft, but after a hard night it would freeze into concrete.

Snow-clearing efforts brought the community alive. Cups of tea were proffered to the drivers. There were exchanges of food, fuel, medicine, anything that might be needed. The young cleared paths for the old. The school children prayed the bus would get stuck on the brae, while they sledged and ski-ed and skated. One year the loch froze so firm that a bonspiel—curling match—was organised. After the road was cleared people came from far and wide, curling-stones were unearthed from cubby-holes and a great day's sport was enjoyed.

Delivering the letters by hand and on foot had given us an inkling, a very small one, of what the 'runners' must have experienced. Post-boys, or in some cases post-girls, rode horses in southern parts, where roads, or at least paths, existed. Beyond Inverness the country was more or less trackless, with bridgeless rivers. 'Runners', who worked for a pittance, were expected to cover up to 30 miles a day, in all weathers, often denied shelter or rest. When one man, weak from hunger and exhaustion, stayed for a few hours overnight in a barn, he was harshly penalised. The runners were often at risk from attack, as it was known that they carried the money paid by recipients of letters which they had to remit to the sending office. Yet it was a job men were glad to take at a time when many were being dispossessed of their land and their livelihood. The path on the north shore of Loch Maree which the runners used to carry mail from the west to Dingwall and thence to Inverness can still be made out and walked.

During the eighteenth century the bags of mail grew excessively heavy as more and more official correspondence and newspapers had to be carried. In 1778 one John Ross, a runner in Inverness, failed to deliver a letter (express) to Thurso, as directed by the postmaster in Edinburgh. Robert Warrand, the postmaster in Inverness at the time, gave orders to 'apprehend and incarcerate his person within the Tolbooth of Inverness and therein to remain until there is advice that the said letter addressed to the postmaster at Thurso is received, to the deterring of others from committing the like in time coming according to Justice.' It turned out that Ross, detained at a ferry, gave the letter to the Tain runner in order to expedite it.

Fighting through deep snow to deliver the post
(Aberdeen Journals Photography)

After a night in prison, Ross, pleading ill-health in the damp and cold, was released on a 'Bond of Caution' for six months, Dr John Alves, physician, agreeing to pay £100 of any further penalty incurred. He must have been a valuable runner!

It's in times of storm that the value of the one focal point which the Post Office represents is fully realised. As soon as a path is trodden through the snow the postie will be on his normal rounds again, calling at every house he can possibly reach. Should he find illness or accident or other suffering in any of the houses he can pass word on to the Post Office, where it can be relayed by phone as soon as the line is restored, or by word of mouth to people beating the snow to collect mail or to cash allowances or buy stamps. Hardship does make for solidarity in any community.

One day, in a time of thaw, after a long spell of frost and snow, a young postie from the town, who was standing in for a sick colleague, found water seeping from under the roof of a house on his route. He knocked. There was no reply. Not wanting to push the letter through the pool of water, he tried the door. It opened easily. To his horror he found a woman lying on the floor. A burst pipe was flooding the kitchen. Being young and nervous, he panicked, and came rushing back to the Post Office. My husband went down. The woman, who lived alone, had collapsed and died. The doctor was called, the police and relatives were contacted.

On another occasion the regular postie, calling on another old person who lived alone, and getting no answer to his knock or shout, tried to push the door open, as he had a parcel to deliver. The door half opened, then stuck. To his amazement, looking down, he found a body lying across the threshold. He closed the door and came at once to the Post Office. We telephoned the doctor. He came quickly, broke a small downstairs window, climbed in and found the woman had had a stroke, but had survived. Arrangements were immediately made, an ambulance summoned and she was soon in hospital. There she was devotedly nursed for some considerable time, but died before she could return home.

Neither of these old people were native to the place. Had they even been returned wanderers there would have been relatives not far away who would have given them shelter or at least have seen regularly to their welfare. There are always those who prefer their independence to soft living, but the going of these two left a sadness in the community. We missed having them come up to collect their pensions, walking in all weathers—rain, frost, fog, all but the heaviest of snow-falls, refusing to take an offered lift, sometimes even a cup of tea. Life, after all, held more for them than one could imagine. Realising this was a sort of inspiration for us all.

VI

A Post Office Library?

With death comes change, inevitably. Houses are sold, newcomers arrive. Would we have young people coming to the office, with family allowances to cash? Would they be commuters, doing business during lunch hour in the town? We could only await developments. Meantime other houses were being modernised, building plots advertised, holiday 'lets' being arranged. Friends were beginning to suggest that we should open a small shop to run in conjunction with the Post Office. But we were reluctant to involve ourselves with the inevitable curtailment of free time, the extra paperwork and so on. I did ask a friend to produce some really good photographs of the area which could be sold as postcards, but the complications of reproduction and the cost were prohibitive.

Close on a hundred years ago there were several 'shops' in the neighbourhood. These consisted of small stocks of dry goods—tea, sugar, flour, salt—kept in the kitchen by a crofter's wife, who made a little profit out of selling them on to neighbours. One place, a little further away, was known as a 'butcher's' because they kept some fresh meat, probably mutton, and no doubt a cut or two of venison. These small stores were of value to the community, especially when the horse-drawn grocer's van from the town was held up by snow and ice in winter. With improvements in communication and better roads they were no longer needed.

'What about a little café?' other friends suggested. Many a time summer tourists, arriving at the door soaked to the skin or exhausted by the heat on their long trek up the hill, have asked desperately where to find a 'tea-room'. In most countries in Europe, they tell us, you can never climb to such a height without finding somewhere to get a drink. 'Sorry' we say 'but come in' to the wet ones, or 'Do sit on the grass' to the hot ones. 'Would you like tea or coffee, or perhaps a glass of cider or orange juice?' In this way we have made many happy friendships, including one with a Frenchwoman who was so surprised at our French and our glass of cider on the green that she invited us to dinner in her flat in the Île St Louis when we went, some years later, on holiday to Paris.

People from many parts of the world would reach our door. We would see them, from the window, drop their heavy packs and scrutinise the name on the letter-box by the road to find out where they had arrived. From the garden we would hear their valiant attempts to pronounce the word 'Abriachan'. The sound of 'ch' stumps even visitors from England! Most often they would then make their way to the door and ask to have their water-bottles filled. I suppose the days have really gone when you could scoop up water in your two hands from a hill burn and drink your fill. Weed-killers and fertilisers, sometimes sprayed from the air, are liable to be wind-borne far away from the plantations they are aimed at and so pollute the most innocent sources of water. Water—that magic element that life depends on—we hand it to them with a smile. They smile back. There is mutual understanding of the significance of this gift.

Those with a little English, looking round, will sometimes exclaim, in disbelief, 'This is a Post Office?'

'It is.'

'But it is...so small.'

'It is. Some people say it's the smallest in the country'.

They laugh. 'So...you have stamps?'

'We have.'

The stamp-book is produced and they look eagerly through it. The pictorial stamps, produced regularly these days, are a great attraction. They buy what they can afford and wave goodbye from the gate.

In the eyes of young Germans, easily recognisable by their accent, we sometimes detect a glint of unease as they identify us as members of a war-time generation. 'We are from Germany' they say. We instantly put them at ease, appreciating their love of wild country, pointing out hill-tracks, lochs for a swim, birds to look out for. These contacts often generate ripples of understanding. One year another group of young Germans arrived, telling us that the hill tracks we had told the first group about are now on a hill-walker's map in Germany!

In these long busy days of summer, with visitors, campers, walkers calling at the door to be attended to, the thought of the office closing is far from our minds. But there is bound to be uncertainty. The place is in a state of transition. Some older people have died, young ones have gone away, to College or University or to find jobs. The houses being built or modernised are clearly for the well-to-do people who will commute to work if they are young or, if they are retired, will certainly have transport and will probably do their postal business, along with their shopping, in the town.

Then, one autumn day, when the summer people were vanishing, we were asked if we would care to accommodate a small branch of the Public Library in the Post Office. We responded with enthusiasm. There would be no kind of salary attached, we were told. No, no, that's all right. There was just room for an ancient bookcase of ours in the porch. Soon we were eagerly awaiting the first delivery of books. Our friends were amazed, as the house was already brimming with books which we lent out gladly. But we were as keen as children to have our own official lending library, with tickets fitted into slots and each borrower having an official ticket to his or her name. These books were to be exchanged by the Council librarians at regular intervals—every three months—and over the years they have sent out a very satisfactory selection of books, fiction, non-fiction and books of all kinds for children.

Each time a delivery was due we would be contacted on the telephone and asked the preferences of our borrowers. Often requests for specific books would be granted, to the delight of the borrowers. We ourselves were privileged to browse through many fascinating volumes. To have them under our roof, close at hand, not scattered over many shelves in a huge building, was a great source of pleasure. I remembered how Alain-Fournier, who wrote the classic *Le Grand Meaulnes*, used to revel, as a child, in the books which his schoolmaster father received for the school library. In our case, the children, in particular, enjoyed being able to help themselves, with no demands for silence! They soon learned how the system worked and became adept at sticking the tickets into their individual cards.

Among the adults we discovered one avid borrower of 'Westerns' and another of 'whodunnits', but few aficionados of Mills and Boon. Most popular was the wonderful selection of books on wildlife, gardening and crafts and biographies. There was no time limit on the borrowing, no 'overdue' fines as long as books were returned before the new lot arrived.

One day, in summer-time again, hearing the door open but no sound of the customer's little hand-bell being rung, I went towards the office to investigate. A man was standing there, staring at the 'library'. He was a stranger, a rather scruffy-looking stranger. A book-lover in disguise, I wondered? As I watched he opened the glass-fronted door of the book-case, examining it as he did so. I realised, then, that it was not the books he was interested in, but the book-case. Catching sight of me, he smiled. 'That's a grand book-case you have there, lady' he said. I recognised the accent— Galway...or Killarney?

'Would you think about selling it? I'd give you a hundred pounds...' His hand was in his pocket.

'I'm sorry. We need it. For the books.'

'You do? And that's some fine books you have there, too.'

'Yes. They belong to the library.'

'Oh, well...' He was looking over my shoulder. 'What about that grandfather clock in the hallway?'

'No, no, that belongs to the family.'

'So you're not needing money? I can give you a good price.'

'I can't reckon these things in money. They're...'

He wasn't listening. His eyes were everywhere, on a vase full of marguerites, on the chair for weary customers. 'The straw chair?' he queried, his voice now with a touch of desperation.

'No, I'm sorry. Why don't you try the place over the hill? There's a village there. More houses. More people.'

Reluctantly, he turned towards the door. 'Goodbye then, lady.'

'Goodbye.'

Feeling slightly guilty at sending him off, maybe to other un-suspecting householders, I watched him get into the van in the yard, where two other men were waiting. These Irish dealers come over every summer trying to buy old furniture and furnishings still to be found in the remaining croft houses. What they manage to buy they sell on at a handsome profit, most often to other dealers over-seas. We have never encountered actual dishonesty in their dealings. They give what is agreed upon, in sound money, and do not steal. But the profit is theirs. And they are very persistent.

Sure enough, a week or two later, coming in from the garden, I again find someone gazing at the 'library'. 'Give you two hundred for your bookcase, lady.' The price had doubled! And word must have spread to other members of the group.

'I'm sorry. I'm not selling it.'

'You'll not get a better offer.'

'Maybe not. But I'm not selling.'

'Och, well. We'll be away next week, mind. See you next year then.' The Irish good humour seldom fails. But I'm thankful to see them go.

I take a closer look at the old bookcase. We had bought it for ten pounds at a house sale some twenty years before, I remembered. It was of oak, glass-fronted at the top four shelves, cupboard-doored below. I resolved to give the glass a clean-up. Was that a trace of woodworm on the middle shelf? I hunted out the bottle of remedy and applied some hurriedly. Then I stood back to have a good look. It certainly was a handsome enough bookcase, though it had never been one of my favourite belongings. Thank goodness, I thought, the dealers hadn't set eyes on my father's knee-hole writing desk or the small mahogany bookcase I really liked.

VII
The Post Goes on Strike

We had been working the Post Office quite happily for some ten years, had grown accustomed to the form-filling, to dealing with customers, to coping with visitors from a' the airts, when we became aware, through the press and broadcasts, that there was growing unease among postal workers in many places. There had been a few 'go-slow' days, of which we had been scarcely aware, the pace of our life not being over-fast at any time.

We ourselves had always felt at one remove from the hurly-burly of the main Post Office life, though we glimpsed it on our occasional visits to Head Office. In our relatively isolated premises, where we were sometimes cut off, in reality, by storm or technical breakdown, we sometimes wondered whether we were actually part of this enormous organisation, with its world-wide ramifications. We wore no uniform. The only official identification of the office was a sign which had become almost illegible from the wear and tear of wind and weather. We liked it thus. As long as our local people knew the way that was all that mattered.

When visiting Head Office we would wonder at the smart appearance of the cashiers in their bright uniform outfits and at their brisk and confident manner in dealing with customers' often complicated requests. Then we remembered those other small, landward offices, where the postmaster had sometimes to be summoned by bells, or a whistle, to come in after office hours to attend to an urgent matter. He would arrive, scrape the dirt from his muddy boots, wipe his hands on a damp towel and leaf through the files to find the official form required. Then, perhaps after a phone call to headquarters to confirm his decision, and a cup of tea in the kitchen, the customer would depart satisfied. We ourselves came into that category of postmastership.

'Unsocial hours' had hardly been heard of in those days. Postal workers of all grades carried on their work largely unsung. Early rising, shift working, overtime was all part of the business. But over the years the demands on the system were getting heavier and heavier. The loads in the postmens' bags were getting heavier, too, clogged up with junk mail of every description. When a chance to work overtime was eagerly seized, that was surely a sign that wages were not adequate to meet the expected standards of life. The hectic rush entailed in coping with the Christmas mail, which was growing greater every year, led to a lowering of morale, bouts of sickness and even absenteeism. So the unease grew and signs of it reached our small outpost.

With our ever-friendly and supportive rapport with Headquarters, our ever-cheerful and indefatigable postie, it seemed unlikely that anything would occur to change the way of things for us. But occur it did—the decision, on 20 January 1971—that there was to be a postal strike. A strike? We knew about them, of course—picket-lines, jeering shouts of 'scab', hardship for the families of those involved. We could do without the arrival and despatch of letters and parcels for a while, but what about funds for our pensioners? There were always enough difficulties for the elderly in the middle of winter.

The first days passed in an eerie calm. With no postman to look out for, the mornings seemed long. There was no exchange of news, no delivery of forms or leaflets, no re-addressing of letters. The stamp book was locked away. The date-stamp remained unchanged. It was as though we were in a time-warp. Was it really possible, we wondered, that all these letters, parcels, documents, newspapers, forms, were no longer circulating round the country, that communication of this kind was at a standstill? It seemed almost like a page of science fiction.

Then the phone calls began. People in outlying places were the first to miss the arrival of the postman, with his bits of news, a daily paper, perhaps a letter. Even a Government form was better than nothing.

'You're not on strike, are you?'

'I'm afraid we are.'

'But...'

The situation seemed totally unreal to him, as it did to us. The Post Office door closed? Surely not.

With the passing days we became almost accustomed to the lack of letters. The telephone was there though the thought of the mounting bill made you stay your hand unless the message was really urgent. Unfortunately, it was not a time for working in the garden. The ground had the ring of frost. Some tidying up left over from the autumn was about all that could be done. Repair jobs, of course, were always with us. Fences, walls, sheds, were in a constant state of disrepair. This uninspiring but necessary work filled many daylight hours.

Always at the back of our minds was the fate of the pensioners. One who rarely listened to news bulletins and didn't have a paper delivered, was the first to arrive. The door was open. It was our own front door.

'I've not seen the post,' our pensioner said. 'Is he ill?'

'No. I think he's all right. But...' We explained the situation. He looked round then and saw that the scales, the array of leaflets, the handbell, everything that identified this small space as a branch of the Post Office was shrouded in a thick grey blanket that covered the table. He drew himself up. He had walked a long way on frozen roads. His frailty was apparent, though he would never admit to tiredness. We knew what must have been in his mind and we understood his reluctance to express it.

'Come away in' I said, 'the kettle's on the boil.'

Over a cup of tea I reassured him. We could pay out pensions at least as long as funds remained. Ater that...the future was uncertain. 'Perhaps it won't last much longer. Next week—maybe...'

'A strike!' he said, shaking his head, slowly, in disbelief. 'Well, well, I never heard the like...'

'It is an exhausting job for many of the postal workers.'

'Exhausting?'

'M'm. Up early, 4 a.m., all the year round for the posties, and the sorting office people hard-pressed, maybe with out-of-date equipment and the shift-work and the pay...'

He was smiling ruefully. I guessed he was thinking of his own early risings, seeing to calving cows or lambing sheep, his long days ploughing, long summer evenings struggling to get a harvest in and then, maybe, everything lost to a storm. 'Well, well...I suppose that's so. Yes. Well, many thanks. I'll be away.'

'See you next week.'

He managed a smile. 'Just so...'

Our unreal situation continued. We could no longer contact Headquarters on the telephone for information or guidance. The lines were dead. Several more pensioners arrived and we honoured their claims until funds ran out. Then, on a visit to town, I discovered, to my delight, that there were members of staff in the accounts department who were not members of the striking union and who could dispense cash, by hand, to sub-offices. In trepidation, I entered the building, after passing through many security devices and check-points. Things were getting unreal again! I handed over the counterfoils from my pensioners' books and received the corresponding amount of cash. This was a great relief. Funding was assured for at least another week.

As time dragged on I made several more visits to the cash department and so managed to keep the pensioners happy. The owner of the grocer's van, who had known the community over the years, would have allowed them to run up bills, we knew. But that was not the way they liked business to be done. Tea and sugar in exchange for eggs, potatoes, or maybe a chicken, was one thing, but for flour, tobacco, a tin of syrup or treacle, for these they liked to pay cash.

Then, one February morning, we had a sudden visitation by several keen stamp collectors from town. The currency had just been converted. The time-honoured old £.s.d. had gone. We were all to think in terms of our fingers. Decimalisation had arrived. The old system—12 pence to a shilling, 20 shillings to a pound—it might have been illogical and tricky for people from other countries to grasp, but it was our own and thus beloved, with all its idiosyncracy. Even the letters—L and s and d—were somehow attractive. Could the amount of shillings to the pound—twenty—have been a recollection of the old Celtic way of counting in scores? Sheep are certainly counted like this still today.

Well, our stamp collectors had acquired First-day Covers for the big day of conversion and would like them date-stamped, please. What could we do? The collectors were people known to ourselves, upright citizens of Inverness. So, quite openly and without a glance over his shoulder, the postmaster changed the date-stamp, gave it a lick and a polish and brought it down firmly on the First-day Covers! That historic date-stamp must still be there, in someone's collection.

Over the years we have built up a stock of first-day covers of our own. Every time a new set of pictorial stamps appears we simply stick them on an envelope and date-stamp them. Most of these stamps are extremely attractive, so attractive indeed that we found it inadvisable to put them on parcels going to certain places abroad as they would be detached by avid collectors and the parcels would be 'undelivered' as 'underpaid'. I often wonder at, and silently applaud, the overall honesty and goodwill of the vast majority of those in the postal service in this country. Occasional cases of blatant dishonesty do occur, of course, but are quickly detected and firmly dealt with.

At last, just over six weeks after it started, the strike came to an end. There was little rejoicing. Our postmen, the foot-soldiers of the service, were hardly better off. The service as a whole was possibly weakened somewhat as firms had to seek alternative means to get their vital correspondence delivered. During the strike the Minister of Posts had waived the Post Office monopoly and had permitted private carriers to handle letters, postcards and parcels, providing they had authorisation from the local Head Postmaster. In this way 300 local services sprang up. Telegraphic communication is useful, but there are always certain documents that have to be studied, forms that have to be signed. In the towns foot carriers took round letters marked 'by hand'. But so much had been missing—the assurance of the safe delivery of even the most valuable of documents or goods, the prompt and assured payment of allowances of all kinds, of postal and money orders, let alone receiving the news of family and friends in far-off places. To live in a time-capsule for a short while can be relaxing, even invigorating, but then comes the urge to break out into reality.

It was early March, the snowdrops were whitening, the blackbird was proclaiming spring from the top of the huge cypress, there was the crying of curlew on the moor, when we heard that things were back to normal. Quickly, we unearthed the stamp-book. Things were perhaps somewhat too normal for our postie. He found himself little better off for the strike efforts, but there he was, smiling as ever. He dumped a huge packet of mail on the table. 'There you are, then. Sorry I'm late. I hope it's all good news. And how are you all keeping?'

'Fine. And you?'

'I'm all right. But you should see the back-log in the office!' He seemed positively glad to be back on the job, whatever the outcome of his absence. That's how it is in a service, which is so much more than a business.

VIII

The First Postal Services

During the days of the strike, when alternative methods of delivering mail were being devised, we thought to take a look back at how the idea of a 'service' to do the job had originated. Like other forms of service, for instance education, which had at first been mostly for the aristocracy, the delivery of letters, documents and so on, had been the prerequisite of the favoured. The unfavoured, of course, could not write or read. The old universities developed means of communication by courier with their counterparts in Europe from the time of their formation in the fifteenth century. The Church, too, had its emissaries Europe-wide and beyond from very early times.

The idea of a regular postal service originated in England in Tudor times with the practice of employing royal couriers for the conveyance of the monarch's mail. Along the more important roads out of London, or wherever the court happened to be, were lines of posts, known as the Royal Posts, marking the way. An official of the royal household, known as 'Master of the Posts' supervised the service. Postmasters were appointed for each stage of the route. They were usually inn-keepers. They were responsible for forwarding the royal mail and for providing horses for the couriers. Post-boys travelled with the couriers, brought back the horses for each stage and served as guides along the tracks.

The first record we have of a royal courier reaching Scotland is that of the arrival of Sir Richard Carey, on Saturday 28 March 1603. Three days earlier, in the small hours, he had left the royal palace near Richmond in Surrey and had galloped north, changing horses at Post-houses every 20 miles or so, to ride into the court-yard of the Palace of Holyrood in Edinburgh and there, on bended knee, to present to King James VI of Scotland the news that his cousin, Queen Elizabeth I of England, was dead.

The sending of letters by private couriers did occur but was not encouraged for fear of plotting against the monarchy. Then, in 1635, Charles I threw the Royal Mail open to the general public. This was the first of the great public services. It was also a way of raising revenue. Strict postal rates were levied and paid by the addressee on delivery, the postage assessed by the number of pages written and the number of miles the missive was to be carried.

Letter rates were as follows:

Single letter:	under 80 miles	2d.
	80-100 miles	4d.
	over 100 miles	6d.
	to Scotland	8d.

Eight pence was a considerable sum at that time.

The carriers of these letters rode their horses at a regulation speed of 7 miles per hour in summer and 5 miles per hour in winter.

Links between Scotland and England increased after the union of the crowns. The need for an extended network of communication, like that in the south, resulted in the establishment of a foot-post between Edinburgh and Inverness in 1669. It operated 'wind and weather serving'. The Receiver of Posts in Inverness was a Mr William Trent. Then, with a growing demand for a better service, at last, in 1695, a fully equipped Post Office was opened in the Scottish capital and soon letters were being carried regularly from there to Aberdeen and then, on three days a week, to Inverness.

Beyond Inverness, as roads were at best no more than tracks, or non-existent, 'runners' were employed to deliver mail. They worked for a pittance and were expected to cover up to 30 miles a day, over trackless country, in all weathers, often denied, as we have seen, shelter or rest.

During the time of the rebellions in the Highlands little progress could be made in the expediting of mail. Sometimes letters arrived, weeks after posting, marked 'Opened by Rebells'. In England things were improving. With the establishment of Turnpike Trusts to help pay for the upkeep of roads made by statute labour, it was possible for wheeled vehicles to run between major towns, and in 1786 the first mail coach ran from Edinburgh to Aberdeen at an average speed of 7-8 miles an hour in summer and about 5 miles an hour in winter.

AN ACT
FOR THE
SETLING
OF THE
POSTAGE
OF
ENGLAND,
SCOTLAND and IRELAND.

At the Parliament begun at *Westminster* the 17ᵗʰ Day
of *September, Anno Domini* 1656.

LONDON:
Printed by *Henry Hills* and *John Field*, Printers to
His Highness the Lord Protector. 1657.

Act of Parliament of 1656 establishing the postal system

A Post Office guard travelled with the coach. Often an ex-soldier, 'accustomed to the discharge of firearms', was employed. The guard was responsible for the safe delivery of the letter-bags. He was equipped with a cutlass, a brace of pistols, a blunderbuss, for use if necessary, and a time-piece for recording the time of arrival and departure at each stage of the journey. There was to be no dallying at the inns! He also carried a horn, used to warn other road-users that the Royal Mail had right of way on the King's highway. The horn was blown, too, when approaching inns, to warn the horse-keepers to bring out fresh horses, which were changed every 10 miles, and when nearing a toll-gate so that the keeper would open up quickly and not hinder the passage of the coach, which was exempt from the payment of toll. Sometimes the mail-bags would be slung over to the inn-keeper without the coach stopping, only slowing slightly. On occasions, the guard, who sat alone at the back of the coach, would be thrown off by the roughness of the road and would blow his horn to draw attention to his predicament!

Many hazardous journeys were undertaken by the old mail-coach drivers. There were hazards for the passengers, too. They were expected to walk up some of the steeper hills, to act as brakes on the downward slopes and to endure all the hardships encountered on the way. Bands of highwaymen would ambush the coaches by blocking the roads with tree-trunks and even ploughs taken from the fields, to cripple the horses. Sometimes ropes would be slung between trees to topple the drivers. The greatest losses were usually incurred by thefts from mail-boxes during the changing of horses. There were other perils—bridges breaking under the weight of the vehicles, runaway horses breaking free of the shafts and, in winter, the ever-recurring threat of snowstorms.

In February 1831 the Edinburgh mail-coach became snow-bound at Moffat. The driver sent one man back to get help for the passengers, then he and the guard mounted the horses and, with the two post-boys, set off towards the next stage. The drifts were too deep for the horses and they had to be sent back. The two men set off alone, carrying the mail-bags. Next day these bags were found, lashed to the post beside the road. The men's bodies were dug out of a snow-drift many days later. They had honoured the watch-word of the Royal Mail—the post must get through. Many similar incidents occurred.

In 1808 the 'Caledonian' coach was running regularly from Inverness to Perth. At stops in Perthshire Neil Gow, the famous fiddler, would entertain the passengers while mail-bags were unloaded. Business was booming and in 1809 a mail-coach was running from Inverness to Aberdeen and the Town Council subsidised the 'Duchess of Gordon' for a twice-weekly run from Inverness to Edinburgh. After about 1819 small, light mail-gigs were venturing further north.

In all these early years of the story of postal communication there had never been an instance of workers in revolt. There had always been a certain prestige attached to the holding of the position of Receiver of Posts. There had been complaints of low rates of pay, but no stage-managed protests. The deliverers of mail were mostly men or boys who were glad of a job, though they worked often in perilous circumstances.

The days of the strike and the introduction of alternative means of distribution of mail had made us think back to these early times.

The alternative couriers of today would have little hardship to undergo. They would be well motorised. Their problem would be to find their way through unfamiliar country and to strange doors in far-away places. We ourselves preferred the orthodox service and refrained from writing all but a minimum of essential letters during the time of the strike. Meanwhile, our forays into the early history of the postal service made us keen to follow these up with the study of later developments.

IX
Mail Buses—a Vital Link

After the long period of strike-led stagnation, the Post Office authorities got busy with an idea which must have been in the pipeline for quite some time—the launching of a fleet of Mail buses. The small red vans with the emblazoned gold crown on the side had always had room for even fairly bulky parcels, even for the old collie dog found straying and to be returned home, even for a ewe spotted injured at the roadside, its mark recognised, to be handed over to its owner for care. These things are part of the day's work for a postman in the hills. Now the new type of vehicle was to accommodate 6 to 8 passengers, on comfortable seats, as well as provide room for parcels, bags of groceries, bread and medical prescriptions in areas where access to shops was very difficult.

The first Highland Mail Bus took the road from Broadford to Elgol, in Skye, in the summer of 1972. It still operates there and has been of tremendous value to the people of those isolated parts, where few other buses run. Its drivers are remembered with gratitude and affection for all their small acts of kindness and help, which often went far beyond the actual scope of duty, giving reassurance to the lonely and the sick as well as practical help to the active and their families. Again, the idea of service predominates. There is a small charge for the ride, but no tipping or extras.

My experience of using Mail Buses has been happy in the extreme. One year I set out for a short holiday in North Uist, having arranged to stay in a small place near a nature reserve, to look at the flowers and birds. Arriving in the evening after a longish sea journey I stayed overnight in Lochmaddy, the first port of call. I was to take a service bus in the morning to my destination. My landlady told me there was a Mail Bus which would take me there if I wasn't in a hurry. If I wasn't in a hurry? One is never in a hurry in the islands!

The first minibus mail service, at Innerwick in the Borders, was started in 1968 (The Post Office)

So, at ten o'clock the following morning I was glad to take my seat beside the driver of the shiny red Mail Bus. 'You're not in a hurry.' It was not really a question. The lilt in the voice meant, I knew, that the idea of time being recorded in hours was meaningless! My destination was to the south, but we went north, through a strange land of moor and bog, with little lochs and, here and there, croft land in bright green patches. We turned off down tracks to isolated houses, waited for a while where a small sign indicated a Post Office and made a stop at the terminal for the ferry to Bernera, Prince Charles's favoured island. All along the way the driver pointed out places of special interest—a crannog on a small loch, the township that was cleared a hundred years ago, where the people still remember the tales of unbelievable hardship suffered at losing their homes and their land, the unspeakable conditions on board the ships that took them away and on the land the survivors found on disembarking. These memories die hard.

'Visitors today—they have their own cars. They come for the fishing or the yachting. They don't know what happened not so long ago.'

'I know. Were some of your people evicted?'

'They were.'

A curlew is gliding overhead. Its flight is beautiful. Its call is sad. Pre-history, recent history, the curlew will have been there through it all.

We pull in to the side as a huge lorry approaches. My driver gives the lorry driver a cheerful wave and we manoeuvre to safety. Coming to a cross-roads, we slow to a halt beside a small red letter-box fixed to a post. A sign on it reads 'out of use'. As I look, a small bird flies out of the opening. My driver smiles. 'It's out of use till the wee bird has reared its young ones.' I smile back. 'You see, there's not many bushes for the wee birds to nest in. The big ones nest on the ground.'

'Yes, I see. That's wonderful.'

'You may wonder about the letters. They're not great letter-writers about here, but if they have one for the post they put a sign at the box and I can call and collect it.'

'So you never know how long your round will take?'

'I have a good enough idea. As long as I reach the airport before the plane takes off. In winter weather I may be held up, but so is the plane!'

From crannogs to airplanes, the island encompasses it all. By the time I reach my destination I feel almost I am no longer a stranger. I risk a thank-you in my halting Gaelic and am rewarded with a far finer turn of phrase and a cheerful wave.

Several times after that I rode in the Post Bus to different and busier parts of the island. Here we picked up many passengers, housewives with bursting bags of groceries, workers from the fish-farm round the coast, campers with enormous rucksacks. Somehow they were all accommodated with much good humour. Their history has left little bitterness in the island people. There's a trace of sadness in some of the old, lined faces, but the eyes soon light up and the hand is outstretched. They positively welcome people from other parts of the world, amazed at the love and concern we feel for their strange land.

'And you have the Gaelic?' they say, wonderingly, as I manage a greeting and a comment on the weather in the 'language of Eden'. I smile. 'Just a little. I wish I had more.'

'Well, well...'

A modern mail bus near Lochinver (The Post Office)

Somehow a Gaelic equivalent to 'Well' has never been devised. The older generation regarded the acquisition of English as essential for their young. The teaching in school was in English. English meant jobs, a better standard of living. Gaelic in the home was strongly discouraged. Only now are some of the present generation regretting this. Affluence can sometimes pall. Gaelic meant the homeland, the freedom to put your own rhythm on the day.

In parts of Canada, where so many island people were landed and left to cope as best they could, the Gaelic language survives, along with the music, the story-telling, the song, the dance. These things must have been essential to their way of life, more essential than their acquisition of 'the English'.

About the middle of the nineteenth century large ocean steamboats started taking mail to many parts of the world. Though there were still many among those who were left at home and among those who went, or were sent, overseas who were not fluent in reading or writing, some form of communication between the two worlds could then be started. As the settlements became established, teachers or ministers of religion could be asked to act as letter-writers for a whole community and their letters despatched to the nearest sea-port. This was a tedious practice but at least it kept families in some sort of touch.

At about that time some islanders, nearer home, were feeling their isolation acutely. In St Kilda, in September 1855, after the crops were ruined by storms, Alexander Gillies, in desperation, despatched several 'mail-boats', with messages telling of the islanders' plight. These 'boats' were hollowed-out pieces of driftwood, attached to an inflated sheep's bladder as a buoy. News of the situation did actually reach the mainland and a rescue operation was mounted. Many of these 'mail-boats', made of canisters, bottles, any type of container that came to hand, were launched over the years. Carried by the North Atlantic drift and the prevailing westerly wind, they sometimes landed in places as far away as Orkney and Norway.

Today, of course, with instant communication by telegraph and telephone, with the whole world connected up by wire, cable and, now, the internet, news of births, deaths and marriages can be transmitted promptly. But these innovations, which were bound to come, have meant that the writing of letters is largely dying out. What a joy it is, rarely experienced now, to come across a bundle of old letters, hidden away in the back of a drawer, carefully tied with a shiny ribbon. There they are, on thin paper, envelopes clearly addressed and bearing the stamps of many countries: Canada, Australia, South Africa, India, New Zealand. Highland people, of course, have found their way to most parts of the world. One hesitates to pry, even at a distance of years, but, at a glance, one can marvel at the delicate handwriting in the delicate prose, the circumlocutions, the whole style of a more leisurely age.

Handwriting, now, has deteriorated to the point of becoming an indecipherable scrawl. I have heard of University students failing exams on account of the illegibility of their papers. The sheer beauty of 'copper-plate' handwriting of Victorian times should make it a recognised art-form. The calligraphy in the illuminated texts of the old books of the monasteries and other sacred texts, dating back 1400 years, is still a wonder today.

I have a neighbour, a lady of 97, who writes the most beautiful hand. She was schooled in the days when such things were important and has practised the art ever since.

X
Visitors from Afar

Over the years we became accustomed to the arrival of strange customers of different kinds, particularly in the summer-time. Most of them were pleasant people, on holiday or passing through, making the buying of a stamp or two an excuse for asking the way. Some of them, particularly those from the U.S.A., would appear quite disorientated in this seemingly wild hill country. They would come slowly from the gate to the door. Then, looking wonderingly round, they would say: 'This is a Post Office, a real Post Office?'

'It is.'

'We saw a kind of a sign. We weren't sure.'

'I know what you mean. It's different!'

Our usual interchange again! We all laugh. It was good, they would say, not to have to stand 'in line', to have time to study the stamps. Often, in the end, they would buy a whole set, stick some on postcards they had bought, but not yet written, and get them date-stamped.

The business done, they settle to discuss the real reason for their visit.

'We're looking for a place called Kirkhill. I guess that means the church on the hill.'

'It certainly does.' I give them a description of Kirkhill and how to reach it.

'Thanks a lot. Gee, I sure am glad we called in to your place. We'll remember it back home. You see, my great grandfather came from Kirkhill. He was a shoe-maker. I guess he made good shoes. We still have a pair he made after he landed in the States. Brogues, we call them. Is that right?'

'It is.'

'He was a Chisholm. So am I.'

I explain about Chisholm country, Chisholms we know and

44

how to look up family records in the archives in Inverness. Contact firmly established, we exchange waves as their car moves off. Some months later a card arrives from Vermont. They found Kirkhill and some Chisholms, though no sign of a shoe-maker.

A hundred years ago there were several shoe-makers in our area. *Greusaiche* was one of the first Gaelic words we had to puzzle over after taking on the Post Office. A letter arrived one day addressed to '*Bail na greusaichean*', difficult to pronounce, but a lovely sound once you acquire the skill. It means the township of the shoe-makers and, sure enough, we were told, there were several men who plied their trade in that part over the years. Good shoes they turned out, too, of hide, strongly sewn and made to measure. Lined with hay for warmth, they would carry you safely over the roughest ground and keep out the worst of the cold and wet.

There was a tailor, too, whose trade is recorded in the name of one of his fields, '*Parc an Taillear*'. He made fine suits of tweed. The story of an area can so often be read in the place-names that linger. The shoe-makers have gone, like the tailor and those who spun and wove to make warm garments, but they have left traces that can still be followed. Someone known as the *breabadair*, the weaver, has never woven a thread in his life, but his father wove before him and is not forgotten.

Weavers, tailors, shoe-makers, they all worked their crofts as well as following their trade. One shoe-maker even found time to work as postman. In the early nineteenth century there was a foot-post from Inverness on alternate days by the north and the south side of Loch Ness to Fort Augustus and thence to Fort William. Letters for Abriachan would have been left at the inn not far from the foot of the hill. After 1840 a mail-cart was tried for a short time, then a daily horse-post, until, in 1876, a steam-boat came daily up the loch. It was at that time that a postman was appointed in Abriachan to collect the mail at the jetty, sort it in his kitchen and distribute it round the area. All this he accomplished on foot. In winter sometimes his tour of duty took him till far into the night, when waist-high drifts of snow barred his way into the out-lying places. One such postman was our shoe-maker. He could only ply his trade when the mail was light, the weather good or in the long summer evenings. Sometimes he got in an hour or two while waiting for the arrival of the steamer down at the waterside, where he had a little shed. The tumble of stones that was his house is still referred to by the few remaining native people as 'the shoe-maker's place', rather than the 'postman's place.'

Perhaps because their trade was a sedentary, indoor occupation, shoe-makers often rendered service to the community as teachers of the young. They would gather a small group of boys about them, hear their reading and their mental arithmetic, tell them the old stories of the clans, and teach them the songs and proverbs handed down through the generations. They would probably hand on a few tips about the making of shoes as well!

It must have been good to see the old paddle steamers sailing up and down the loch, carrying people going about their business, goods, potatoes, many other things besides the mail and calling in at various points for loading and unloading. At one time juniper berries from the south side of the loch were taken aboard and ex-ported to Holland for use in the making of gin. The loch was busy, with real purpose. Now the jetties have rotted away. A few trawl-ers go through, fulfilling the original purpose of the great canal-builders—to make a safe passage from east to west. There is an anchorage for pleasure-boats and some noisy water-skiing goes on on the south side of the loch. There is a fish-farm there and, of course, hordes of motorists in the parking places along the loch shore, looking for the mysterious creature that lives in the deep.

The daily steamer carried the mails till well into the twentieth century, then the last one, the *Gondolier* of happy memory, was put to rest as part of the Churchill barrier in Orkney. The great Caledonian Canal, of which Loch Ness is a part, is in dire need of repairs now. We hope, desperately, that funds will be found to keep it working. The building of it by Telford in the early 1800s was an engineering feat of the first order. The work involved, by men delving with pick and shovel and carting earth and stones in barrows, is unimaginable. They were accommodated in wretched huts, but they earned a little money which was welcome. Some-times they had to be severely dealt with when they walked off the job at harvest or sowing-time to attend to matters on their crofts. Their superiors lived in good stone houses which still stand. The children go swimming, now, and dive off the broken jetty in the bay where the steamer used to call.

One question our summer customers inevitably ask, after their drive up from the loch shore, is have we seen the 'monster'? Though I travelled that road twice a day, five days a week, to my work as a teacher, I had never seen any sign of an unusual creature in the water. I had long ago come to hate the use of the term 'monster', which seemed to designate something not only huge, but ugly, forbidding, in fact, monstrous. People we know who have, without doubt, seen a creature in the loch, describe it as sinuous, long-necked, graceful even, as it occasionally emerges and submerges. One young woman I met, minutes after a 'sighting', the wonder of it still in her eyes, described the head of the creature as like that of a Cheviot sheep. It had been as real to her as the sheep on the croft where she lived. Another sighting was described to me by a man on a place close to the loch shore. He had just climbed on to his tractor and started up the engine when, looking up, he glimpsed something long and black and sinuous disappearing below the surface. Clearly, the noise had disturbed the creature. He stopped the engine and waited till the small waves of the wash broke gently on the pebbled shore. Neither of these sightings were revealed to the press.

One stormy day in autumn, towards late afternoon, a customer arrived who was not going to ask about any strange creature we might, or might not, have seen, but to tell us about strange things that, he reckoned, had been going on in our area for countless years.

'This is the Post Office?' he wondered.

'It is.'

He made no attempt to buy a stamp. 'You've been here quite a long time? You know the area quite well?' It was more as though he were telling us these things, not asking.

'Yes...we've been here getting on for thirty years. That's nothing, of course. You count in hundreds here.'

'Hundreds? Millions, I should say.'

I laughed. 'You're right, if you count the rocks.'

'I do. Tell me, do people living here have a reputation for longevity?'

I thought of the hearty nonagenarians who worked their ground. 'I believe they have.'

Some sort of rapport with this strange customer was beginning to emerge. I looked at him more closely. He was dishevelled, with a scruffy beard, a mud-stained jacket hanging loose on a thin frame. Glancing over his shoulder I could see, in the lay-by, an old van, bashed on the side, an untidy pile of equipment sprawled on the roof.

'Have you a map of these parts—?'

'Yes. Will you come in? My husband will show you what we have.' He knocked the worst of the mud off his boots and followed me into the sitting-room. 'A cup of tea?...or coffee?'

'Thanks. Tea, please.'

I poured a big cupful and handed him a scone. A full dinner was what he really needed, by the look of him. But hunger was clearly unimportant to him, as long as his mind was satisfied. He took a long drink, then, taking out a small magnifying glass, he began to pore over the map.

'You know...there's a big stone, just up there, at the crossroads, with markings on it?'

'Yes, I know it.' I passed that stone almost every day and had often looked at the markings. 'The marks are not cup-marks, I think.'

'No, no. Cup-marks were made by humans. These go way back in what we call time. Now, look. Here, on a map of today we can read things about the past. See the line of the stream, the contours of the hills. They tell us something of what has been going on below the surface. All this pre-dates the existence of humans. But they followed, the early ones, they followed instinctively, the ways they felt were right.'

'So that stone was a marker?'

'I believe it was. And this house...it stands very nearly on the line pointed out. That's why I had to come. And your garden, up there. There are marks all over your garden.'

'Really?'

'Really. These old ancestors of ours had a good inkling of what the world was all about. We've lost so much of what they learnt. We've covered everything, almost everything, in concrete. True, we've built palaces and towers, but take one flower, one autumn crocus I saw by your gate, and—you remember—Solomon in all his glory...'

For the first time he was smiling. He folded the map and stood up. 'I must go. Thanks for the tea.'

'Are you camping?'

He laughed. 'I just doss down in the van.'

I saw him to the gate. The sky was clearing to make way for the first stars. He looked up.

'You know, I think a day may come when this old earth re-asserts itself, maybe joins forces with the planets and sends us all tumbling into space. Let's wonder at it all for a while, anyway.'

'Yes, indeed.'

I watch as his rickety vehicle lurches up the road. We never saw him again, but what he said haunted our minds for long. Working the garden ground in spring I felt a strange sense of awe as I thought of the origins of that substance which we'd tamed to serve our needs. We were clever at taming, but there were forces we'd never overcome. Had we invented our gods out of fear, setting up palaces for our kings, placating our overlords with offerings we could ill afford? Perhaps our 'customer' was right to go around the world in poverty, looking for signs and wonders, telling of them to those who'd listen.

In summer, walking the moor ground where we always looked for the hut circles that told of human habitation, realisation came to us of the vast underlying sources of energy we could feel in our bones. Of course, we said to our inner selves, this is why we feel so well. We can partake of this energy. It's better than any meal. We thought of our 'customer', his thin frame and his immense vitality. 'More things in heaven and earth', perhaps? We were glad the Post Office had brought him to our door.

XI
Changes, and the Voting System

We had been in the schoolhouse/Post Office for rather more than ten years when Jim's health began to give us cause for concern. He was so strong, wiry, resilient, always so cheerfully ready to tackle anything, had never had a day's illness in years, his worst pain an attack of lumbago a long time before, so that to think of him as incapacitated in any way was almost impossible. But even the hardiest frame has to give way some time. He developed osteo-arthritis. Pain-killers did nothing to alleviate the suffering. He was taken into hospital for a general 'assessment' of his condition. Hospital in the beautiful days of June was anathema to him. I was trying to make arrangements to get him home, with or without 'assessment', when he had a stroke and did not recover.

I was glad that his last years had been busily happy. I had taken early retirement from teaching so that we could share fully the work of the Post Office and looking after the house and garden and 'curating' the museum which we had been involved in over the years. Our daughter had married and two small grand-daughters had been trotting in and out of the house and playing in the garden, to his great delight. His going left a great blank in many lives, not least in those of the community of which he had been a part and where his nature had been fully appreciated. He had always made time for people, time to talk, time to listen, time to have a joke, to help where he could. The young people who came about working on projects liked his sense of humour, the very old appreciated his kind approach.

In due time the Head Postmaster came to see me. In those days we had a Head Postmaster and he came quite often to visit. Now we have an Area Manager. He is probably snowed-under with paperwork,

50

as all administrators are today. Contact is less frequent, but we have regular visits from other supervisors.

On this occasion the Head Postmaster had time to sit down, to talk quietly and to ask me whether I wished to take over the Post Office duties officially. If I did not, he said, it would be quite understandable, but it would probably mean the office would be closed. Closed? Surely not! I thought of the shoe-maker, cobbling away while he waited for the steamer, sorting the mail on his kitchen table, taking it round on foot, in all weathers. I remembered the five other houses, some still known as 'the old Post Office', where letters had been posted, stamps sold, orders cashed, news exchanged. No Post Office? I thought of the men, and one woman, who had carried the mails in our time—close on thirty years. They were all crofters with places of their own to see to—crops, sheep, cattle—people who could turn their hand to many jobs. Now we were modernised, the mail arriving at our door ready sorted, in a shiny red van, but surely not modernised to the extent of shutting the Post Office, the only focal point for the area, since the school had been closed for nearly twenty years and no-one now ran a shop.

I looked at the Head Postmaster sitting there, with the power in his kindly hands to mark the end of an era. I had an idea he was aware of that and was quite glad when I said I thought I would like to keep the Post Office going. He got up with a smile and said: 'Well, now, think it over and let me know in a day or two what you decide'.

He had always been more of a father-figure in our lives, rather than a boss, someone we liked and respected and did not need to fear. He had always been interested in our books, our museum activities and forays into local history.

It didn't take me long to make up my mind. I had been initiated by Jim into the ways of filling in returns, working out the balance, ordering stock and so on. The Post Office must stay. The place must retain its identity. Abriachan was known in song and story since the days of Columba's settlement at Kilianan, down on the shore of Loch Ness. It had been church land, had provided sanctuary for the persecuted. Part of it had once belonged to the far-famed Wolf of Badenoch. Its inaccessibility had allowed for the concealment of stills and the production of sellable drams, when money

51

had to be found to meet the rising cost of rents. In the 1920s its children had made the name Abriachan synonymous with excellence in Gaelic singing.

It is no longer inaccessible, but it retains much of its special character. Large areas of moorland have been afforested but some native trees remain—birch, rowan, hazel, alder—and on the lower slopes, oak, holly, hawthorn. There are still enough patches of heather and bracken to gladden the eye in autumn with the glory of purple and gold. The rocks still shine, the granite and whinstone that built the first solid houses of stone. The water still cascades into the big loch down below, forming deep brown pools and providing power to run a dynamo for the nursery garden on the shore. The name Abriachan is said to mean the confluence of the speckled burn with the water of the loch.

Montrose's troops had passed through the Caiplich area, just to the north of the Post Office, on their way to make camp near Beauly. They had made themselves unpopular, as soldiers do, by carrying off cattle on their way. Skirmishes took place. The 'battlefield' can still be made out. No doubt the troops dined well that night, but the quiet people would have lost a large part of their livelihood. War always overides normality. Andrew de Moray, the great Scottish patriot, was here, too. He and his men ambushed the governor of Urquhart Castle on his way from Inverness and inflicted damage on his cavalcade. Wounded men from Culloden had passed this way, too, limping back to their homes in Glen Urquhart. These things were often in my mind as I walked in Caiplich, where our crofting days were spent.

Next morning I was up early, gave the date-stamp a thorough cleaning and brought it down vigorously on the daily despatch form—ABRIACHAN. We were lucky, I knew, to have our own named stamp. Most small offices in the area came under the umbrella stamp of Inverness. Old-fashioned our equipment might be, but we liked it that way. The stamp-book was held together by the good workmanship that must have gone into the making of it. In the back flap were labels of amazing antiquity. There was a set of delicate bronze weights for the delicate bronze letter-weighing scale. I was surprised, one day, to see in the Inverness Museum a parcel scale, the exact replica of the one we had in everyday use. It serves its purpose very adequately and no one is in the greatest of hurries here. The weights go on and off and on again till the exact figure is worked out.

Our nursery gardeners from the loch shore who often have a number of parcels of plants for despatch and scales of their own, have everything ready-weighed so that we only have to check them and work out the cost. This is a great saving of time and the plants get away fresh. So...this morning—it was a bright blue summer morning—I looked round the little office, at the clear word Abriachan on the despatch note, at the old stamp-book still holding together, at the sturdy old scales, at the books on the library shelves. I looked round again. Then I went to the phone and spoke to the Head Postmaster. 'I'd like to stay on' I said. He was happy with my decision and I duly signed the Official Secrets Act—what official secrets would come my way, I wondered?—and was sworn in.

Some time previously I had been co-opted on to the Community Council and it was to be my privilege to serve on it for a number of years. We met, originally, in a very small hall, known as the 'hut', some 5 or 6 miles nearer to Inverness. In winter we wore our heaviest clothes as the heating was minimal. Getting home, when frost had turned the snow to concrete, could be tricky. But it was good to be able to discuss the problems affecting different areas—road maintenance, rights of way, water supplies, facilities for children and pensioners.

Latterly, meetings took place in a big, warm room at a nearby school, which was more congenial but lacked something of the intimacy of the early days. It was always difficult to make the general public aware of the importance of having a Council near to them, anxious to hear of their grievances, to do things to help. Attendance at open meetings was always poor. However, with the re-organization of local government, the Community Councils are, I think, coming into their own as a valid link between people and power.

One of my duties as a Council member was to organise the election of members which was to take place at regular intervals should more than the requisite ten put forward their names. In fact, this rarely happened. My appointment to this duty came about because it was known that my husband and I had always organised the voting for elections of other kinds—local, parliamentary, even, once, a referendum. This voting took place in the big schoolroom, just through the wall from the house and the Post Office. Elections always seem to happen on a Thursday, which was half-day in the Office, so little disturbance was caused. I would put a notice on the house door, telling customers to use the school door. Then I would take the necessary equipment for the morning duty through to the schoolroom.

Some time before Polling Day I had swept and garnished the place, fixed the polling booth, filled the coal scuttle, brought in some vases of flowers. Then I went to town to fetch the ballot box and all the necessary equipment. Over the preceding days party workers had been busy, sticking notices on telegraph poles, bushes, trees, in valiant efforts to get the voters to the poll.

On Polling Day I was up by half past five and into the schoolroom to light the fire, back to snatch a quick breakfast and to fill flasks of tea and coffee. Then the Post Office equipment was taken in and when by seven o'clock my assistant, the polling clerk, had arrived the fire was burning brightly and we were ready for our first voter. The sealing of the ballot box was an incredibly old-fashioned process. We fumbled about with red tape, wax spills and sealing wax till it was secured to our satisfaction.

With only about 80 voters on the register we knew that we would not be rushed, but the long day did loom ahead of us. Over the years different people have been sent as assistant to the Presiding Officer, the title I rejoiced in. All have been congenial companions and have helped to make the day pass pleasantly. The first people in to vote were always the commuters on their way to work in town. Some were joggers who came extra early, trying us out to make sure we hadn't overslept, they would say, with broad healthy smiles! There would be a lull, then, till after nine, when the local bobby would look in, just to make sure everything was in working order and running smoothly. We assured him we had no problems, offered a cup of tea and saw him off with a 'see you later' smile.

The postie would arrive at his usual time, well briefed about the slight change of location of the Post Office. The routine office work was soon accomplished.

'I've been reminding them all about the voting. It's a good day. They've no excuse!' With his usual cheery wave he'd be off, to jog more memories on his way.

By mid-morning we were ready for a coffee-break. If we were lucky there'd be just time to quaff a mugful between voters. A few people found it convenient to buy a few stamps after voting. I knew all our voters by sight so when a strange head appeared round the door we realised it was a party worker or an election agent, just sounding out the ground, reckoning up the turnout. There was no exit-polling with us. We would just smile at the anxious faces and make a polite comment about the weather. We had always been lucky with our electorate. There were no problem voters, no handi-capped or blind people, just the occasional proxy voter.

By late morning another lull would set in. The Post Office closed and the apparatus was locked away. I brightened up the fire. Even in summer there's a chill in the old schoolroom. I turned on the radio to hear news of polling over the country as a whole. Munch-ing our sandwiches we listened intently as word came over the air of the numbers who had voted. I did a quick count of ours.

'We've had 35 so far!'

'But remember, that's nearly half the electorate!'

'You're right. The percentage is quite good!'

In early afternoon another bobby would arrive to make sure we had no rioting. Rioting? We asssured him all was quiet!

'Not too quiet, I hope?'

'No, no. Just normal. How are they doing down the way?'

'They're quiet, too, they say.'

'We've had nearly 50 per cent in so far.'

'You're doing fine, then. See you later.'

As the next hour or so passes we begin to feel slightly drowsy, the early start to the day beginning to tell. I brew some good strong coffee in an old pan on the fire and we revive. Then what amounts almost to a 'rush' occurs. Some older people arrive, driven in neigh-bours' cars, a young mother with a child in a push-chair; another bringing an older child, just home from school, to let him see how voting works. I remember how, in our early days here, we went to some of the most outlandish places in the area to fetch people to the polls in our old ramshackle vehicle.

Things brighten up fast. Tea-time brings returning commuters, some we haven't seen for long enough, as they tend to buy stamps in town. Greetings are warm, news is exchanged, they meet up with people they also haven't seen much with the busy lives they lead.

'It's almost a party!' one exclaims. 'Why don't we do this more often?'

The laughter and the cheer revive us. The pile of voters' cards on the table is rising. We check the number again. We listen to the 6 o'clock news. The evening is long. Another bobby arrives, a sergeant this time.

'Any problems?' His smile is wide, his presence welcome.

'None at all, thanks.'

'You'll get the box back to town all right?'

'We will.'

We're secure in the knowledge that, should there be a breakdown in our arrangements he will see to transport. Contact with the police, our Highland police, is always reassuring. They are there, always, to help. Strong, courteous, always totally reliable, if they have to make arrests, that too, is a help. Many of them are from the croft lands in the west, some are Gaelic speakers, all of them understand the people, the country and its ways. You find them in the big cities, too. Along with engineers, doctors, vets, they carry their own special brand of integrity.

After a supper snack we begin to look out the numerous forms which have to be filled in before the box is despatched. Nine o'clock comes. Another news bulletin. The sound of a tractor outside just drowns the reader's voice. I switch off.

'Sorry I'm late. The cow was calving'.

It's a neighbour from the heights. Apologising for his grubby hands he wastes no time in making his cross and slipping his paper into the box.

'It went well?'

'Aye. A bonny wee heifer.'

'That's good.'

There are more important things, even, than voting. A lastminuter arrives, with no excuse, only a dash and a wave and a closing door. Ten o'clock and the poll is over. Before fatigue clouds our brains we do the last calculations together, checking each other's results, complete the forms, I sign everything, we close the hole in the box, with sealing wax and red tape again, parcel up all the stationery and equipment which can be used next time and we're ready for the road.

The counting-house is a lively place—bright lights and bright people at the long tables, eager to begin their task. Our box is checked in and we retreat. The result of the count in our widely scattered area will be long in coming. Reaching home I switch on the television, watch for a few minutes and fall fast asleep. The cat wakes me, jumping on my knee. I stagger up to bed, listen to the radio for another few minutes and have to give in. The Post Office must be open in a few hours time.

XII
More Visitors

The little museum next door with which I was involved brought people of many different types, some of whom came to the Post Office to buy stamps and to linger for a chat. Most of them were genuinely interested in the old artefacts and the glimpses of a former way of life which they gave. Many were knowledgeable and contributed a lot to our own understanding. Some of the elderly men of crofting background, for instance, were able to explain to us exactly how a horse-driven mill was worked, something we had never seen. Some visitors were a little strange.

One large, portly gentlemen, with an unmistakeable German accent, asked me:

'Please, can you tell me, where is Elgin?'

'Elgin? Well, it's quite a long way from here. Have you a map?'

'Yes, I'll get it from the car. You see, I am a geologist. I want to see those Elgin marbles.'

I try to suppress a smile.

'But...they are not in Elgin. They're in London. In the British Museum.'

'Oh! How is that?'

I try to explain about Lord Elgin and Greece and....it's difficult. He goes away, not totally convinced, I feel. But then neither am I.

Another day, a young couple, mid-European this time, I judge, looking perplexed, ask: 'Where is castle, please?'

Mid-Europeans often leave out the definite article. 'A castle?'

'Yes. We see picture of it in Tourist Office. Where Queen comes. Here, on my map. I show you.'

It's a map of the area. I look. Underlined, in pencil, is the word 'Balmore'. I smile.

'Oh, that's a common place-name. It's from the Gaelic, turned into English—"bal", a collection of houses, and "more", meaning big. We have Balbeg, too. That means a small collection of houses.'

They listen intently, their faces falling.

'Oh...so Balmoral not here.'

'No. It's a long way away. In Aberdeenshire.'

'Oh, and what is here, please?'

'Well, here we have just the hills and the trees. People don't work the small fields much now. But...'

The listeners' eyes brighten.

'Oh, that is good, isn't? So you have not much what is it? Pesticides?'

'You're right. That is good. We still have birds. Not as many as long ago. But still...'

'And flowers. We see them by the road.'

'Yes. A good lot of flowers.' I begin to feel we can really compete with Balmoral. Then comes the inevitable question.

'And have you seen monster?'

'No. I...'

'But it's so near, big lake. You can see it almost from your door!'

'That's true. But we have a small lake here. Just up the road. We call it a loch.'

After several valiant attempts they achieve a remarkably good pronunciation of the word.

'You mean there is also monster?'

'No, but...' I embark on the story of the kelpie, the water-horse of legend. It's difficult with their limited understanding of the language, but gestures help, and their co-operation, their willingness to understand.

'Oh, we go there, then. And we see birds. And flowers. Thank you. Thank you.'

I point out the road and wish them well. No castles here, but birds and flowers. I scan the sky. Not a golden eagle, maybe, but buzzards and curlew, swifts and wheatear and at the loch there will be sandpipers, maybe dragonflies skimming the water, and the scent of myrtle and meadowsweet and the little white rose. I envy them their walk. Their memories will be happy.

People from the U.S.A. are often amazed at some of our postal arrangements. One large gentleman, wearing a large Panama hat, and a very large smile, came slowly up from the gate.

'My, you have a pretty garden. And is this really the Post Office?'

'It is.'

'I thought so. We saw the letter-box over the road. But there's not much of a sign.'

'No. But people know.'

He laughs. 'They have second sight maybe?'

'Some of them have!'

'And I guess your mail-man would have to have it to find some of the places he has mail for. Some are way off the road. In the States we have a box at the end of the side-road, even at the end of the garden path, at the gate, for the letters to be deposited. And a place for parcels, too. The folk can collect them at leisure. That saves a lot of time and wear and tear on the delivery vehicle, I reckon.'

'I'm sure it does, but here people like to have a visit from their postie. Especially those who live alone. And they mostly don't have mail every day.'

He smiles. 'You folk like a touch of feeling in your services, I guess.'

'Well, yes, if you like.'

I venture into a homily of my own.

'About a hundred years ago it was decreed by Queen Victoria, no less, that every household in the country should have a free delivery of mail. It was to celebrate her Jubilee.' His eyes are wide.

'What d'you know? Well, well. The old lady did you proud.'

'She did. Before that you had to collect your mail at the nearest office or pay to have it delivered, sometimes by people of doubtful honesty. But, of course, this nation-wide delivery did mean problems in the Highlands and particularly the islands.'

'You can say that again. Imagine taking a letter to some place in the Isle of Skye when the ferry couldn't operate on account of a storm. And there was no bridge, like now, and no airplanes. Oh, my!'

'And there were places much more remote than Skye. All the Outer Isles. And the islands of Orkney and Shetland. Now, of course, everything goes by air.'

As I speak a deafening noise from overhead makes my visitor cower.

It subsides. He straightens up.

'Sorry about that,' he apologises, 'it reminds me...well, never mind.'

Probably Vietnam, I think.

'Well now, I've enjoyed our talk so much. I guess I'll buy a stamp or two.'

I produce the stamp book and leaf through it.

'Your stamps are so pretty. I like them all. But I guess some are a bit big for my postcards home. I write such a lot on them about your lovely country. There's no room for big stamps.' After much careful choosing he makes his purchases and pays up, with a satisfied smile.

'You like it here. Have you, perhaps, forebears from the Highlands?'

'I haven't but my wife has. She's back in the States. So I reckon our kids are half Highland, bless them. No, my folk came from Austria. They had to get out. I've heard about Highland people having to get out, too. 200 or so years ago. Is that right?'

'It is. A lot of them were forced out of their places to make way for sheep. The clan chiefs had become more like landlords than father-figures and wanted to make money out of their estates.' '

Yes. That's what I heard. It was known as the Clearances, I believe.'

'It was. That's how there are so many people of Highland descent in Canada, Australia, New Zealand and...'

'And the States!'

'That's right. Some of them did leave voluntarily. Things were bad at home and they hoped for something better elsewhere. But it took them a while to find it.'

'And now? How are things now?'

'Getting better slowly, I think. But the huge numbers of sheep that were imported and then the red deer that were allowed to breed unhindered for the hunting fraternity, have done so much damage to the natural environment. It will take years to recover.'

'I can imagine.'

'But we have people working on it, here and there.'

'More of your pioneering spirits! That's good to hear. I'll be telling the folks back home where to come when they're in Scotland. I guess for the price of a stamp or two I got good measure. Now, goodbye. God bless!'

There's the trace of a jaunt in his step as he goes back to the car he left in the lay-by.

Another time, a bright summer day, brought us a family from Canada. Three children came racing up the path, bright eyes dancing in sunburnt faces. They reach the door and burst in.

'This is a Post Office?' It's the disbelieving tone we're used to.

'It is. Would you like a stamp?'

'We have no money. We'll have to wait for Dad.'

'He made us walk up. He's coming in the car.'

'Told us he's walked the road so many times. He was at school here.'

'He was?' I get a word in. 'Would you like to see inside the school?'

'Oh yes!'

I fetch the key and open up the schoolroom. They look round wonderingly.

'Did Dad really study here?'

'You can't see out the windows.' The small girl shivers.

'It's kinda spooky.'

'I know what you mean. That's because it's been empty for a good while. When there was a fire in the grate and lots of children at their desks it was fine.'

'Dad must have learnt something. He's an accountant now.'

'A very good one.'

'I'm sure he learnt a lot. He'd certainly know his tables. And he'd have no calculator to do his sums for him.'

'Tables? What do you mean?'

'Maybe you don't call them that. It's...multiplying in your head.'

They laugh. 'That's funny—multiplying in your head!'

' "9 9s are 81, 9 10s are 90"! We were always so glad when we got to the tens. That was safe ground. And we weren't allowed to use fingers for adding!'

We turn. Their father is standing in the doorway, smiling, savouring the atmosphere.

'Can you still multiply in your head, Dad?'

'I can. And I can add without using fingers. And...' almost talking to himself, 'I can say poems. "Young Lochinvar, he came out of the west". It's handy when you're on your own, on a journey. It brightens up your thoughts...' He comes back to earth. 'It's great to see the old place again.'

'Where was your Sports Field, Dad?'

'Sports Field? We had the playground. And we played football in a field over the road. And shinty.'

'Shinty?'

'Yes. I guess I've a lot of explaining to do. Now let's say thank you to this lady.'

'And can we buy some stamps?'

'Of course.' I get back behind the counter and open the stamp-book.

'These are lovely ones. Can I have a set, please, Dad, for my collection?'

Dad obligingly opens his wallet. My stock diminishes alarmingly. I make a rapid note of re-stocking needs.

'Come on, kids. We've got a long way to go yet.'

'It's only a flying visit?'

'Afraid so. But we'll be back.'

'I'd like to stay...' the small girl looks sad.

I make up a bundle of Post Office leaflets and put them in her hand.

'Would you like these to remember the Post Office?' She smiles.

'Yes thanks. My friends at home would like some too.'

'Good.'

'Goodbye' comes in chorus as they turn towards the gate.

'Goodbye' I call, and 'haste ye back.'

'What does that mean?'

'Your Dad will tell you.'

'I sure will.'

The car roars up the road. '9 9s are 81' and 'Young Lochinvar'... I'm glad they've survived those long years and miles.

XIII
Supervisors and Surveyors

During our twenty years in the Post Office we had had comparatively few visitations by officials from the Head Office. The accounts people had kept a check on the books, of course. A young man would appear at the door, briefcase in one hand, his identity card in the other. In the sitting-room I would clear a space on the cluttered table, bring in the cashbox and stamp-book, make up the fire if it was wintertime and settle down discreetly in a corner while he did his adding up, on his calculator. On one occasion when the result came out, alarmingly, with quite a large cash shortage, it was decided to do a recount. To my great relief it was discovered that one of the small dockets from a pension-book had attached itself to another. It was unstuck and the sum was duly rectified. When everything was checked and checked again we exchanged smiles of satisfaction and I went to make coffee.

Subsequent re-organisation of the postal hierarchy has meant that we have quite regular visits from an area supervisor who comes, not to check our business, or our ways of conducting business, but to see to any needs we may have, to listen to suggestions. This attitude is very welcome. The people at Headquarters have always been there, of course, helping out with problems of all kinds, sending emergency supplies of cash or stamps following some unexpected demand, explaining the filling-up of new, unfamiliar forms, their friendly voices on the phone always reassuring, though we never met. Now an actual personal contact was established we felt less isolated. Once, when the lock on the cash-box jammed and pensions were due a locksmith was sent 'post-haste' from the town to sort the problem out.

In older times a most important position in the Post Office was that of Surveyor. In 1789 Francis Ronaldson was appointed Joint Surveyor for the whole of Scotland. The work involved was arduous in the extreme. Covering hundreds of miles, mostly on horse-back, sometimes by coach, over unmade roads, in all kinds of weather, would have tested the stamina of the strongest man. Ronaldson was of small stature, but a great personality, with a strong sense of humour. As a member of the Royal Edinburgh Volunteers during the Napoleonic wars, he almost disappeared when on parade among his taller comrades. He had a specially light musket made for him! The salary, on appointment, was not high—£150 a year, plus a subsistence allowance when travelling of ten shillings a day. Later, salary and allowances were increased owing to the special circumstances of travel in Scotland, the Highlands in particular. Scarcity of mail-coaches meant that private vehicles or horses had to be hired and inn-keepers charged their highest rates to Government officials.

Surveyors were expected to keep a full record of all their journeys, commenting on the standards in the various offices they visited. Their accounts also served to justify the amount claimed for subsistence and travel allowance. Ronaldson's journal from 1786 to 1814 has survived, giving a valuable picture of the working of the Post Office and of the abuses by serving officers and by the public which it was his duty to uncover and remedy.

The Surveyor, who represented the 'eyes and ears' of the Post Office, often found himself unfairly blamed for lack of vigilance when things went wrong. Things did quite often go wrong. Many postmasters, who were also inn-keepers, were sometimes busy attending to customers and indulging in drink, with their postal duties handed over to illiterate servants. Occasionally they practised deliberate fraud, forging 'dead' or mis-directed letters, postage on which could be deducted from the sum they had to remit to the head office. The low rate of pay accorded to the postmasters was the main reason for their yielding to the temptation of the many opportunities for dishonesty with which they were presented.

The actual carriage of the mail was arranged by the postmaster, with a mileage rate allowed, and delegated to runners or riders—'Post-boys'—who received five shillings a week, the postmaster keeping the surplus. Thefts of mail inevitably occurred when boys of 14, ill-clad and underpaid, had to cover distances far beyond their strength. Punishments in those days were severe in the extreme. Erring Post-boys could be imprisoned or deported. In 1796

A Post-boy riding at full gallop in about 1800 (The Post Office)

the postmaster in Kirkwall was executed for the theft of £9 from letters.

The public, too, indulged in dishonest practices. When the custom was for postage to be paid by the recipient, the actual arrival of a letter would be enough information for the addressee, who would refuse to take delivery and thus avoid paying the postage.

Franking—the free carriage of letters through the post—was another custom which could lead to abuse. It had long been the privilege of M.P.s, the Commissioners of Supply and certain other public servants to use this service. In the nineteenth century several poets and novelists, whose work entailed a fair amount of correspondence and whose financial situation could be precarious, made good use of the franking system. Shelley is known to have profited by it and Sir Walter Scott, in a letter preserved for posterity, refers to 'Mr. Freeling, G.P.O., who gives me the privilege of his unlimited frank in favour of literature'. Francis Freeling was the Secretary of the Post Office.

All these things, and more, made the Surveyor's task a difficult and, in some cases, a distressing one. Francis Ronaldson must have seen many facets of human life as he travelled the country—the whole of the mainland and as far north as Orkney. This wide travelling enabled him to perform another important part of his duties—the seeking of alternative and improved routes for the carrying of the mail. There were problems. Freeling, the Post Office supremo, knew nothing of the geography of Scotland, or of the climactic conditions found there, the severity of storms, blizzards and ensuing floods. The landowners, particularly in the Highlands, still maintained a feudal authority and, with the increasing volume of mail which they despatched and received, were insistent that the delivery should be routed to suit their convenience. Only by constant pressure on the authorities in the south, headed by Freeling, did the Surveyors for the north, Ronaldson and, later, James Shearer, manage to get some sort of justice for the Post Office servants—the postmasters, the post-boys, runners and riders and the operators of the mail-coaches.

There were other problems. In 1832 a serious outbreak of cholera affected the whole of Scotland. Runners were refused entry into many places for fear that they carried infection. Mail bags had to be fumigated and routes altered.

Anthony Trollope, who worked for over 39 years as a postal Surveyor in the south, wrote, later in the century, about his life's work: 'You have married no wife, keep no hunters, go to no parties, read no books, but have become a machine for grinding and polishing Post Office apparatus. This is not good enough for any man, though there are worse ways of spending life.'

Freeling had written of the Surveyors: 'The Surveyors must be of respectable description, high character and unexceptionable integrity and of good education. The salary and allowances are not equal to the constant duty, trusts and responsibility and expense.'

Anthony Trollope is, perhaps, the Post Office figure best known to posterity. In a Minute to the Postmaster General dated 4th November 1834 Freeling, the Secretary to the Post Office, wrote: 'I beg to submit...the name of A. Trollope as a junior clerk in the Secretary's Office. Mr Trollope has been well educated and will be subject to the usual probation as to competency.' Many years later, in his autobiography, he described how he entered Post Office service and worked out his probation. As a handwriting test he copied a page of Gibbon which was never inspected: a threatened arithmetic test was never applied. During seven years at Post Office Headquarters he was underpaid, neglected and largely ignored. He felt morally degraded and a professional failure.

A chance vacancy for a junior official in the west of Ireland, for which he applied in despair, was to prove his salvation. Subsequently, during his long years as a Surveyor, with the sensitivity of the artist, he observed and sympathised with the hardships of the postal workers. Accompanying a Glasgow postman on his delivery round, climbing tenement stairs, he recorded that this was the hardest day's work he had done in his life. He also pointed out that 16 miles a day should be the greatest distance required of a foot-post. Trollope was also a keen advocate of the idea of a free delivery of letters to every house, which did eventually materialise. He fulfilled his Post Office duties with energy and drive and at the same time managed to pursue a successful career as a writer. His mother had written novels. This may have spurred his ambition. His travels up and down the country, his meetings with people of all kinds would have provided a rich source of ideas which he was able to develop while he rode or rested at inns. He was a prolific writer and his books are read by many thinking people today.

Nowadays, with smooth roads through the glens and routes mapped in the skies, the Surveyor's job is quite different. He, or his equivalent official, can reach the furthest outposts of the business in a matter of hours. He has few travelling problems to contend with, but still complaints have to be heard, complaints by postmasters about lack of funds, complaints handed on by customers about the occasional lost, delayed or damaged letter.

When he, or she, appears out of the blue, we greet him, or her, no longer with apprehension (did we fill in that new form incorrectly?) but with relief, knowing that he, or she, will listen sympathetically to our request for a new cash-box or a rack to display the ever-increasing number of leaflets for distribution to customers. With my concern for the rain-forests of the world I'm always pleading for a reduction in the supply of these leaflets, but it seems there is a standard quota for each office. At least I hope the recycling unit is in good working order. Our Surveyors of today are certainly good listeners and do understand the problems of postmasters working in the comparative isolation of a country office.

XIV
Read All About It—in the Post Office

When the grandchildren came to stay at holiday time the place became lively indeed. A toy Post Office, in a box with fake stamps and postal orders, was no use to them. They had the real thing. When 'Postman Pat's' shiny red van was glimpsed from the window there would be a stampede to the door and out to watch him empty the roadside letter box. 'Steady on, now' I would call. They were sure of a cheery greeting from our friendly postie, which they reciprocated energetically. Then, quietening down, they would watch with bated breath to see what was in the delivery. Bills, receipts, advertising material, anything at all was exciting when it came straight from the hands of their uniformed postman. When he had letters collected on his route, for posting, their privilege was to lick the stamps for him. The date-stamp was the greatest thrill. In off-duty hours they were allowed to practise using it, on odd scraps of paper.

On a visit to town they would wander round the big Post Office shop, with its somewhat forbidding grilles and uniformed staff. With holiday money to spend they were spoilt for choice in the bright array of things on show. The Post Office does look after the interests of its young and future customers. Models of Postman Pat were of no special attraction to these particular young customers who had a real one to hand, but bright postcards, colouring books and letter-writing outfits were well worth spending pennies on. This needed no encouragement from me. After their return home I was always thrilled to find small envelopes in the post, stamps carefully fixed, the address in best handwriting, with small items of news on the paper inside.

The Post Office encourages letter writing by organising a competition with quite valuable prizes for school children in various age groups. I always hope that competitions like this may do away with that ghastly comment 'boring'—applied by so many young people to so many activities such as letter-writing. The grand-daughter who enjoyed our little post office the most, who once date-stamped her own hand, which must have been extremely painful, has developed, I'm very glad to say, into a writer of most attractive letters. Like her mother before her, she spent quite a lot of time abroad, as a student, and, again like her mother, found time to write at some length and in distinguished handwriting, letters of real interest. These I keep tied, not in ribbon, but in stout rubber bands. She also liked to receive letters, thus encouraging others to try their hand at this art. I firmly believe letter-writing can be con-sidered an art-form. What is it but the spontaneous expression of thoughts and feelings committed to paper at a certain time, in a certain place, thoughts and feelings about people and events as well as thoughts and feelings directed to the recipient of the letter? Isn't this what the painter does in his picture, showing us what he thinks and feels about his world as he fills his canvas? The poet, too, bar-ing mind and heart in the lines he writes, hopes we will catch a glimpse of his meaning. Letters, pictures, poems are surely all means of communication. And calligraphy is certainly a form of art.

The Post Office also sponsors events of literary significance. Every summer, at the Edinburgh Book Festival, a huge tent, in the gardens of Charlotte Square, hosts lecturers and writers of distinc-tion who speak about their work and inspire many apprentice writers. The function of the Post Office has always been more than that of carrying letters. Today, as we have seen, it is a focal point for small communities where neighbours can meet and local news is exchanged.

During the eighteenth and nineteenth centuries, when the whole country was desperately anxious to hear about the events taking place, not in their locality, but on the continent—the French Revolution, the Napoleonic Wars—the Post Office became a place for the reading of newspapers. These were sent to the postmaster ready franked, that is, without payment on receipt, and he was able to make a small profit by charging customers for reading the paper. As many people were unable to read it is likely that a liter-ate member of the community, probably the school-master, would read the news aloud to the assembled company. In the days of the mail-coaches people would gather at points along the route shouting for news from the guard or other out-riders. These would shout back and this verbal exchange would sometimes lead to distortions of the actual news. In case the distortion might lead to panic or disaffection the authorities in London and in Edinburgh thought it prudent to issue, from time to time, hand-bills giving a correct account of events, sending them to postmasters with instructions to distribute them in their towns or villages.

For example, one such issued in London on 10 February 1817 ran thus:

> The statement in the morning papers that several persons have been arrested by warrants from the Secretary of State is true. The meeting was held this morning in Spa Fields, but the arrests which have taken place and the precautions adopted by Government caused everything to end peaceably and the town is perfectly quiet.

Today, we have no mob-quietening devices in the sub-post offices—we leave that to the police!—but we do act as information-gathering centres. A small fee is paid by the local government for the display of planning applications for houses or buildings in the vicinity. The Register of Electors for the area is held in the office and many notices on a variety of subjects—accounts of Community Council and School Board meetings, lectures, sales of work, meetings of all kinds—are pinned up on the notice board.

XV

Love Letters and the Penny Post

All during the eighties I kept the Post Office going, juggling my duties there with hours spent curating the small museum next door, seeing to the chickens, the goat, the bees and the garden. It was a busy life, but it never palled.

New and very attractive stamps were appearing at regular intervals along with corresponding postcards. My pile of home-made first day covers was growing steadily, as was my collection of cards. These I found too attractive to send away. Some day they must go into an album. The artists employed in the designing of these stamps and cards are of high calibre.

The Post Office first thought of issuing cards in the late 1880s. Later they were issued commercially and after that there was a deluge. Some people were slightly apprehensive about messages going out unsealed, to be read by all through whose hands they passed. Mostly, the cards bore only short greetings. Today, they are sold in large quantities in holiday resorts, but are not in everyday use. Those produced in the Highlands at the present time, depicting landscapes and wildlife, are of exceptionally high quality. An album collection of them could well be made to delight the eyes of future generations, when perhaps most greetings, holiday or otherwise, may well be transmitted electronically.

Meantime, the profusion of greeting cards for every occasion—birthday, wedding, retirement, illness, sitting of and result of exams and so on and so on, and of course, Christmas—augurs well for the sale of stamps. As I marvel at the design and colour of each new issue I think back to those in my old childhood collection, still lingering somewhere in a cupboard, for the grandchildren to inherit. How dull most of those stamps are, compared to today's,

Sir Rowland Hill, the great pioneer of the Penny Post

though they did teach us a little about the world, at least how to recognise the native names of countries—Helvetia meant Switzerland, Suomi was Finland, Magyar stood for Hungary and so on. My most longed for stamp—which I never acquired—was, of course, the Penny Black. Some Penny Reds I did inherit later.

Hunting out that old album and studying its contents made me curious about the origins of those old Penny Blacks, with the gracious silhouette of the young Queen Victoria. She was a great letter writer and keeper of journals, I knew. I dug out the story.

In 1836, one year before Victoria came to the throne as a girl of 18, a schoolmaster's son named Rowland Hill happened to spend a holiday in a village in the north of Scotland. (He was a member of a Society for Popular Education and had much sympathy for the poor.) There he witnessed a scene which touched him deeply. A letter from London arrived for a village girl. The postal charge was great and she refused to take delivery of it, though she knew it was from her fiancé who was working in London. The couple had devised a system of signs and marks on the cover of the letters he sent which let her know that he was well and that he loved her.

Profoundly disturbed by this story Hill gave much thought to the matter. He concluded that the vicious circle—in which high postal charges caused a diminution in the number of letters carried and this then forced the rate up in order to make a profit—must be broken. In 1837 he published a pamphlet, *Postal Reform*, in which he explained his proposals and also pointed out the enormous social advantages which even the poorest would enjoy. He proposed 'small stamped labels' to be sold in advance and attached to the letter by the sender. A committee was formed and more than four million signatures were collected in support of the project. Hill made great efforts to influence public opinion. The Post Master General, the Earl of Lichfield, opposed the plan vigorously.

However, in September 1839 Hill was given a temporary appointment at the Treasury, where he could supervise the introduction of his reforms. He managed to get the support of the progressive elements in Parliament. A letter from his brother at that time says: 'That a stranger should be bold enough to attempt to penetrate the mysteries of our postal service was something which those who had the professional charge found disagreeable, but that he should be so successful was even worse!'

Hill's committee, which consisted of twelve London businessmen, published numerous pamphlets. One they called *Examples of Postal Charges in 1839, to be preserved as Curiosities in Museums*. There is no doubt that postal charges in the years after the end of the Napoleonic wars were excessively high, being looked on as a form of taxation. Ways of avoiding them grew more and more ingenious.

The committee issued posters, as political parties do today. One proclaimed:

> Mothers and fathers who wish to have news of your absent children: Friends who are separated and wish to write to each other: Emigrants who do not want to forget your motherland: Farmers who want to know the best places to sell your produce: Workers and labourers who want to know or find the best work and the highest wages—support the Report of the House of Commons by your petitions in favour of the Uniform Penny Post.

Eventually, the Prime Minister, Lord Melbourne, put it to the vote, the proposal was carried and on 10 January 1840 the Penny Post was established. The huge cut in postal charges resulted, of course, in massive bottle-necks of mail at the post office counters.

A competition was held, the public being invited to submit

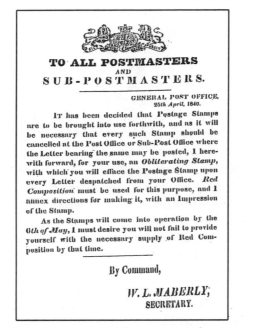

TO ALL POSTMASTERS
AND
SUB-POSTMASTERS.

GENERAL POST OFFICE,
25th April, 1840.

IT has been decided that Postage Stamps are to be brought into use forthwith, and as it will be necessary that every such Stamp should be cancelled at the Post Office or Sub-Post Office where the Letter bearing the same may be posted, I herewith forward, for your use, an *Obliterating Stamp*, with which you will efface the Postage Stamp upon every Letter despatched from your Office. *Red Composition* must be used for this purpose, and I annex directions for making it, with an Impression of the Stamp.

As the Stamps will come into operation by the 6th *of May*, I must desire you will not fail to provide yourself with the necessary supply of Red Composition by that time.

By Command,

W. L. MABERLY,
SECRETARY.

The announcement of the new stamped postage

designs for the proposed stamps and envelopes. The winning envelope depicted Britannia sending winged messengers to all parts of her vast empire. This design was subsequently ridiculed and withdrawn. The stamps, however, were a great success. They bore the effigy of the young Queen Victoria, her crowned head facing left. The penny stamp pre-paid postage to any part of the United Kingdom on a letter weighing up to half an ounce.

A grateful nation raised a subscription to Hill amounting to over £15,000, Parliament granted him a gratuity of £20,000 and he was eventually made a Knight Commander of the Bath. He died at the age of 84. On his statue outside the G.P.O. in London are the words 'He created a Uniform Penny Post 1840.' Hill could never have envisaged the world-wide spread and development of the stamp he had created. One hopes that the young couple in the north of Scotland who helped to inspire his work took advantage of the new rates and were eventually re-united.

XVI
The Acceleration of the Mail

The Post Office, like any large organisation designed to be of service to the public, has, of course, to be subject to many changes over the years. In our small outpost we saw those changes, as it were, at one remove. We were aware of what was going on and were kept well informed by documents emanating from headquarters at regular intervals, but we saw comparatively few of the changes in action, since our customers were not numerous and their needs did not vary much. As long as they got the stamps they needed (and most were not great letter-writers), the occasional postal order, the occasional parcel posted (though both these items had become increasingly expensive), and pensions and giros cashed, they were happy. Telephone, Hydro-electric and, later, community charge bills they were glad to settle locally, thus avoiding queues in the busy offices in town.

We were aware that Royal Mail and Post Office Counters had separated, but this might have happened on the moon for all the difference it made, in reality, to us. Our postie still arrived in his smart red van—red the colour of royalty—with the golden lettering and the golden crown on the side, wearing his smart navy uniform. We were conscious, perhaps, of our own dowdy appearance, as we stood behind our 'counter'—wearing normal working clothes, using our tattered stamp-book and clumsy scales. We were quite happy that way, preferring old, well-made equipment to modern, more flashy devices. We resented a demand for the obsolete brass letter-weights to be sent to a postal museum somewhere in the south. We treasured our museum pieces, especially our own named date-stamp. When the old roadside letter-box went the same way, replaced by a modern version, we began to fear for the old red phone-box up the road. So far it is still with us. When it was our duty to empty it I would sweep and dust it regularly and hang bunches of myrtle to keep away the flies. Phone-boxes in the wilds hold happy memories for me, of shelter from rain-storms and blizzards, even of somewhere to cook sausages on a spirit stove, out of the wind, on camping holidays! The care of the box is now in the hands of other workers.

The Post Office is always striving to improve the quality of its service, with independent research companies monitoring the mail delivery performance over the country. A customer service is in operation to deal with enquiries or complaints and questionnaires are often sent out inviting comments. Increases in the cost of services is announced well beforehand. A Post Office Users' Council is ready to take up really serious complaints regarding delay or loss of mail, though the Recorded Delivery, Registered and Registered Plus services should obviate most complaints.

A vast amount of effort has gone, and goes, into ensuring the satisfaction of users by assuring the safety and increasing the speed of delivery of items posted. This has been going on for many years. On 14 December 1758 a letter from the post office in Edinburgh acknowledges receipt of a letter about the 'slow progress of riding the mail between Aberdeen and Inverness' and the 'great remissness of duty in the several postmasters entrusted with the execution of that service.' On 13 March 1710, in a letter to Alexander Duffy, Provost of Inverness, about complaints against Alexander Cumming, Deputy Postmaster at Inverness, it was said that there had been 'intercepting, delaying, opening several letters sent in the bags of Inverness to the great prejudice of Correspondence and the diminution of this branch of her Majesty's Revenue.' Several gentlemen of Inverness were to enquire into the problem.

There were problems too, with the safe carriage of goods. In September 1747 Mr Thomas Wedderburn of Inverness wrote three times to the storekeeper at the Excise Office stating that there had been 'this long time complaints that our stores were much spoilt in the carriage'. Thereafter they were to be sent otherwise, that is, by Alexander Calder, Carrier, who is to go eight times a year from Inverness to Edinburgh at £16 a year' and 'he is to get two boxes with locks and a wax cloath to lye over them: so we expect to have none of them spoilt as before was often the case.' The temptation must have been great to have a taste of the cargo on the long journey south!

In 1798 a mail coach from Edinburgh to Aberdeen at last started running, though Francis Freeling, the then newly appointed Secretary to the Post Office, considered that, on the surveyor's report, 'the state of the roads is highly unfavourable for the passage of coaches.' There were worries, also, about the crossing at Queensferry, particularly in the winter months.

That same year the 'Memorialists', that is people writing 'memorials' or memoranda to the authorities, were complaining bitterly that 'letters from the south and west and their foreign correspondence are detained eight hours daily in Edinburgh, whereas the official duty necessary for forwarding them does not require a detention there of more than two hours.' Apparently business was done at a leisurely pace in Edinburgh, with the fashionable hours for dining strictly adhered to.

The previous year Alexander Allardyce, M.P., had written that 'the mortifying neglect with which their applications and remonstrations...have been treated by the Post Office have...resolved, as their ultimate resource, to bring the matter before Parliament.' Francis Freeling, based in London and ever anxious about the profits of the Post Office, had perforce to listen to his Surveyors in the north who knew the country well.

In 1803 work was started on the construction of the Caledonian Canal. The improvement of Highland roads and bridges also went on apace and this naturally facilitated the running of the mail coaches. The north was coming to be recognised as a region of importance to the economy of the country as a whole. Yet in 1822 there were still cries for the Acceleration of the Mail. William Blackwood, in Edinburgh, printed a 'Plan for expediting the Mail London to Edinburgh' so that 'It shall arrive at 10 o'clock on the 2nd day (and eventually earlier), proceed immediately for the NORTH OF SCOTLAND and cross at the Queensferry all the year in Daylight'.

When the coach was scheduled at seven miles an hour the coachmen often stopped at the ale houses and loitered, then drove too fast. Accidents occurred. With the improvements in the roads they could do nine miles an hour. To save time they would hand over the mail-bags without stopping, merely slowing to an adequate speed.

Much debate went on about the best route between London

Mail coach handing over mail bags to a postmaster in the 1840s
(The Post Office)

and Edinburgh. Telford, the great engineer, was asked to advise. Finally, in 1823, a committee was appointed to obtain an 'Acceleration of the Northern Mails'. Through the 1830s, 1840s and 50s the efforts to expedite the delivery of mails continued. With industrialisation in the south, the development of the fisheries in the north and so on, there was urgent need for an efficient postal service.

At last, in February 1864, the Provost of Inverness received a letter from the G.P.O. saying that mail would be carried by rail as soon as the necessary preparations were completed. In 1866, when the Highland Railway was in operation, 'memorials' of complaint were still flying about. One, from the Town Council of Inverness, on the old topic of 'acceleration', now referred to the 'Acceleration of Mail Trains' and was to 'receive consideration'.

Ten years later a speed-up was still being demanded. From Inverness to Aberdeen the train ran at 19½ miles per hour, whereas from London to Perth the speed was 39¼ miles per hour. In 1881 a letter from Alan Cameron, Provost of Elgin, to Provost Fraser of Inverness stated: 'Train service between Inverness and Aberdeen disgraceful: 20-30 minutes wasted at Forres and Keith: takes nearly six hours to travel a hundred miles'. Could there have been specially welcoming refreshment rooms at Forres and Keith? Perish the thought! It must have been a question of dilatory loading and unloading.

The Railway Company was clearly eager for trade but it had a lot to learn in the operation of its service. Drivers had to be taught to handle machinery and to keep to strict standards of discipline. Once, at Christmas time, on the Inverness to Nairn line, the driver and fireman were both drunk and quarrelsome and were dismissed on the spot.

The transition from mail coach to train took time. Initially, the whole coach, with mail-bags on board, was transferred to the train, along with the guard. The problems of travel were not over. Even sturdy engines, with sparks flying and smoke belching from the funnel could, and did, get stuck in snow, which banked up on the line. And there were no 'post-boys' to stagger ahead through the drifts with the bags of mail. The 'Acceleration' was well and truly hampered on those occasions.

It was still not adequate for people in the north even in normal circumstances. In 1881 a deputation of fifteen landowners, most of them M.P.s, led by the Duke of Sutherland, went to London to meet the Postmaster General, Mr Fawcett, to urge the necessity of an improved mail service to the north of Scotland. They pointed out that Aberdeen had 'the advantage of a special mail-bag engine from Perth to take forward the London mails at a high rate of speed'. They wished to have the same for Inverness, Wick and Thurso. Mr Fawcett agreed that an improved service was highly desirable, but made it clear that cost was the important factor and asked these worthy gentlemen to use their influence in getting the Railway Company 'to meet the department in a liberal spirit'. The ball was neatly back in their own court!

XVII
Servants of the Public

Today the Post Office is firmly resisting attempts at privatisation. It is still essentially a service, though, of course, it must find the means to pay its way, as its great eighteenth century Secretary, Freeling, did. Even he heeded the advice of his Surveyors, men of great humanity, who knew the country well and were able to stand up to the fierce demands of economy in practice coming from the south. They knew only too well the frustrations of the grossly underpaid servants of the Post Office. The postmaster's job, in particular, seemed to be in many ways an unenviable one, having great responsibility attached, for little pay and the threat of heavy punishment for misdemeanor. Yet the position of postmaster was still attractive to many. It gave the holder a certain standing in the community and kept him well-informed about events in the country at large. It seems to have counted in its ranks mostly people of basic integrity and worth.

These days we have a chance to meet our counterparts from a fairly wide area at conferences in Inverness. Transport is arranged for those who don't run cars and we meet in a comfortable room in the hotel built on the site of the old inn which used to see off the 'Caledonian' coach with the mail to Edinburgh. After the initial greetings and exchanges of news our sense of isolation disappears. We realise afresh that the folk gathered here have the same hopes and fears as ourselves—hopes that the business in our small offices can be maintained, fears that our identity may be lost as we are, perhaps, swallowed up in amalgamation with bigger places. Small country schools are closing. To modernise and equip them all with the new tools of technology would be too costly. To modernise and equip our little offices—would that be impossible? Probably. But I think our customers don't really notice the state of our equipment as long as we're there when they need us and have the supplies they're looking for. Our 'passing' customers, tourists and holiday people, positively appreciate, I suspect, our lack of sophistication and the fact that we have time to pass more than the time of day. Computerisation may be in the air, but I put the thought of it to the back of my mind. Our supervisor has not, so far, hinted that it is imminent.

Modern devices are certainly to the fore at our meetings, clipboards much in evidence, of course, and screens flashing up information at the touch of a button. But the talk is on an informal level and we are all encouraged to give our views on proposed developments as well as to air criticisms and complaints. Even the 'airing' is salutary, though we know that most grievances must go, if not unheeded, at least unresolved. On the whole we do not complain overmuch. We know the rules. We are, by nature, inclined to respect them. Our work is not stressful. We can soldier on till well past normal retiring age if we feel so inclined, knowing that we are not keeping anyone younger out of a job, for the work is home-based and devoid of glamour. In a neighbouring glen two sisters ran the Post Office from their croft house, one at the counter and the other taking the mail round on her bicycle, till they were both in their nineties. In another, a postmistress of 87 has just had a presentation in recognition of her sixty years in the job and has no thought of retiring.

Looking round the company at these meetings, I see men and women of widely differing ages. Some will be running their offices in conjunction with a shop. Some will have taken over after the death of a spouse. They all seem to have the same sense that what we are engaged in is a form of service. We have rules to stick to, but we can, sometimes, go out of our way to help. When a young man walks straight through to the kitchen, where I'm making jam, at seven in the evening, demanding one first class stamp, I turn down the heat, wash my hands and unlock the cupboard. 'It's an application for a job' he says. 'That's fine. Good luck to it!' A smile lights my jam-smudged face.

Our local imbiber has been known to arrive home in a hired car, stumble up to the door at night and demand a 'sub' on his pension to pay the driver. This was in my husband's time. 'I can't do that, man,' he had to say. Then he would delve into his own pocket. 'You can pay me back on Thursday.' These small acts help to humanise the great institution that does depend so utterly on the integrity of its servants.

The faces I see at our meetings reflect that sense of loyalty. There's humour in them, too, love of a good joke as well as the appreciation of the stark realities of life. Contact with people at large certainly makes us all aware of the wider world out there. The relief on the face of a young mother, her husband unemployed, as she cashes the family allowance and the money goes straight into her own hand—that is a look to treasure. Pensioners, too, show relief as they pocket some actual cash, though some of them still appear slightly diffident, as if to accept the money, however well-earned, is like admitting to poverty. This was a thing abhorred by Highland people. Poverty was hidden till relieved by the shared generosity of one's own kind, generosity which could be repaid when another's need arose.

So, the business of the meeting ended, we exchange experiences and comments and find much strength in the renewed sense of solidarity among ourselves and with the powers-that-be, at least the local ones, in this huge organisation.

XVIII
William Dochwra and 'Indian Peter'

The postal service has thrown up, in one way or another, some characters of amazing strength and originality. During the eighteenth century, when, with standards of education rising, and more people able to read and write, the demand for communication facilities was growing, a Londoner, William Dochwra, organised a system of delivery of mail which he called a 'penny post'. This was a form of protest against the high rates of postage charged by the official authorities.

In several hundred taverns, coffee-houses or stationer's shops, the public could leave letters and packets to be collected and sorted. 'Penny Post' messengers would then deliver them, five times daily in the suburbs and fifteen times daily in the city. This 'Penny Post' soon became so popular that it posed a serious threat to the monopoly of the official post office. After a legal action brought against him, Dochwra was fined a hundred pounds and ordered to cease operation. Eventually, his idea was taken over by the Post Master General and he was awarded an annual pension of five hundred pounds for ten years.

At about this time Peter Williamson, a remarkable Scotsman, came on the scene in Edinburgh. His story is as remarkable as himself and is worth the telling. He was born in Aberdeenshire in 1729 and was sent by his parents to an aunt in Aberdeen, where he went to school. In those days there was a busy trade in African negro slaves, supplemented by a more discreet enterprise—the kidnapping of young children to be shipped to the plantations in America, supposedly as apprentices. Peter was playing along the quayside in Aberdeen one day when he was decoyed on board a ship, then seized and pushed into the hold with about fifty other children.

On the voyage they suffered indescribable hardship. Arriving in the teeth of a gale, the ship grounded in Delaware Bay, the captain and crew taking to the boats, leaving the children to their fate. Next morning, the storm abated, they returned to the ship to salvage the cargo and found the children had survived.

Peter was sold for £16 to a Scottish farmer in Philadelphia, who had himself been kidnapped as a boy. This farmer treated Peter well during the seven years they worked together. When he died he left the boy £150, his best horse and other goods. This enabled Peter to marry and acquire a strip of land. But in an attack by Indians, who sided with the French, his wife was murdered, his farm burnt and he himself carried off as a prisoner. Eventually escaping, he enlisted in the British army, was wounded and imprisoned in Quebec. When finally released he returned to England, landing with six shillings in his pocket.

All this he wrote down. On his way north, stopping at York, he met a kindly gentleman who gladly undertook to have this account of his adventures printed and circulated 'for his benefit'. With the small profit made from selling his book and from impersonations of Indians on the war-path, he was able to complete his journey to Aberdeen. On arrival there he lost no time in accusing one of the City fathers of being responsible for his kidnapping and that of other boys and was soon arrested, fined and turned out of the City as a vagrant.

Now nick-named 'Indian Peter' he made his way to Edinburgh, where he opened a tavern known as 'Indian Peter's Coffee House', in the hall of Parliament House. He next moved an action against Aberdeen Corporation and was awarded £100 compensation and costs. While his luck was riding high he opened another tavern— 'Peter's Tavern'—in Old Parliament Close, which did so well that he was able to open a bookshop and printing house in the Luckenbooths, near St Giles.

Here, in 1774, he printed an *Edinburgh Directory* in which he stated:

> The Publisher takes this opportunity to acquaint the Public that he will always make it his study to dispatch all letters and parcels, not exceeding three pounds in weight, to any Place within an English mile to the East, South and North Leith every hour through the day, for one penny each letter or bundle.

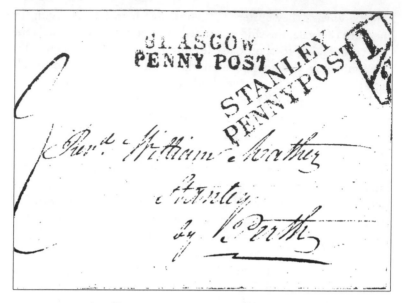

*An envelope showing the marks of early Penny Posts—Glasgow
and Stanley in this case*

The letter-carriers were called 'caddies' and wore hats with the words
'Penny Post' on them. Letters were postmarked to show whether
the postage had been paid by the sender or was to be collected on
delivery. The business flourished and Peter was able to marry again
and bring up a family. He later divorced his wife, she declaring that
he had left her destitute.

'Indian Peter's' Penny Post, although a challenge to the monopoly
of the official organisation, was allowed to continue for close on
twenty years. Thereafter it was taken over by the Edinburgh Post
Office and Peter was paid a pension of £25 a year as compensation
for the loss of his business. 'If you can't beat them, join them'!

In the following years local Penny Posts were established in
many parts of the country. They worked smoothly and were fast
and inexpensive. Their success was no doubt an inspiration to
Rowland Hill in his work in establishing the official Penny Post in
1840 and in the regularisation of the costs of postage from which
we all benefit today. So 'Indian Peter', with his colourful life, has
earned a niche in the story of the postal service and in the social
history of the country as a whole.

XIX
Abriachan in the News

Our post office is small, there is no doubt about that. In fact, it seems to grow smaller as time goes by and the piles of leaflets and official documents, some in large plastic folders, grow ever larger. I am often guilty, too, of cluttering the corner by the door with the odd garden tool as I come in in a hurry after a spell of digging or weeding. As I sweep out the stone floor and polish the old brass door handle I often realise how much I treasure it as it is, warts and all.

But just how small it is and how it must strike other people sometimes was brought home to me one morning when a reporter from the town, looking for a story, arrived at the door. He stood there, gazing round, scrutinising everything as news reporters do, his facial expression growing into amazement. I waited. Then he said: 'I reckon you must be the smallest post office in the Highlands.'

'You think so?'

'Well, I don't know how they can get any smaller!' Very soon he was into superlatives of all kinds. I began to think this must be the smallest post office in the country, if not in the world! 'I'd like to do a piece on it. D'you mind if I send out a photographer?'

'Well, I don't...'

'It won't take a minute. The photographing, I mean.'

'Well, I...' I seemed to have no defences handy.

Next morning, sharp at nine, the photographer arrived. Taking in the set-up in a couple of glances he quickly re-arranged all the movables, turning the table round to catch the light, piling the weights on the scales. 'Have you a parcel anywhere? It could look as if you're weighing it.'

Feeling completely out of my element and into something phoney, I obey his instructions like an automaton. When all is posed to his liking a young assistant appears with a huge reflector which he holds at an angle to the picture. The feel of unreality grows. At last, the eye of the camera is glaring at me. Panic strikes, but I hold firm, as though trying to outwit an enemy.

'That's great!' There's reassurance in the tone. Then: 'Just a minute. A little bit this way. And again. Now we'll just try once more. To make sure.' The clicking goes on and on. I look up. Two people are waiting outside. They smile.

'I didn't know you were in films!' one said.

'Neither did I!'

We hurriedly put the post office together again. I deal with the customers, the photographer packs up his equipment and life gets back to normal.

The piece did appear in the paper. It was quite well done and the photograph was passable. But this was not the end. Stories are picked up here and there all over the world of journalism, I suppose. It was not long before another photographer was sent out by a well-known Sunday newspaper and our little place became part of a feature on rural post offices all over the country.

Some time after that I was able to breathe a sigh of relief when I heard that someone in a village over on the other side of the loch had opened a post office in her broom cupboard. Her *broom cupboard*? That must make hers smaller than ours, I reckoned. And so it proved. Hers featured in a television broadcast and in a magazine in Canada, so we were let off further reportage.

Nevertheless reporters continued to come out from time to time. Knowing our long-standing interest in the history of the place, they would come looking for 'stories'.

'Any illicit stills about these days? Any poaching? Sheep-stealing? Come on, you must know!'

They seemed to have a total disregard for the effect any disclosures might have on the people involved in unusual activities of any kind. It's only when you live in a small community that you understand the great value of discretion.

We knew of no stills in action, though we had friends who made many a bottle of first-rate wine—rowan, elderberry, birch-sap. We knew where the remains of the old bothies were. We had heard many a good story about the ingenious ways the gaugers had been outwitted. That was history.

Poaching? Well, if you heard the echo of a shot coming through the still air over the hill on a spring evening you might think to yourself 'that'll be one for the pot'. But it could just as easily be a keeper from the Forestry Commission out to kill some roes or getting a fox before he got the lambs. As for the fishes in the small loch up the road, well, you can take them from the bank and no one can stop you, but sadly there are so few fish since the surrounding hill was planted with conifers, the fertilisers have washed down and the water now sprouts greenery of various kinds.

Sheep-stealing? Now, that's a thing that can only go on at night, surely. We do sometimes hear heavy vehicles in the small hours, but most often we just turn over and go back to sleep. Only our vigilant police will have an idea about a crime as serious as that—one which was punished by hanging not so long ago—and they will exercise all the discretion their job demands.

Our communities' peccadilloes are as nothing by comparison. A dog allowed to roam the countryside may be impounded, a neighbour's sheep are hounded out of garden crops, but certain codes are strictly kept. Gates have always to be shut, fences not climbed for fear of damage, no lighted matches dropped, sheep, cattle or horses found straying are rounded up and herded to safety. Adherence to rules such as these keeps the community going along happily, but they don't make headlines. Most often our visiting reporters have to be turned away, after a cup of tea.

One story which might well have been a scorer I kept under wraps with the utmost vigilance. Quite often someone would come to the door asking for eggs, or milk, or other country produce, thinking the houses were farms. One slightly dishevelled young man appeared one morning with such a request. He was living in a shelter he had made from pine branches just up the hill, he said. Invisible neighbours like him are welcome. I gave him what I could and wished him well. He loved the solitude, he said, in impeccable English. A poet? I hoped so. What a wonderful way to spend a summer, I thought—walking all day, having the time to look at things, at birds and mosses and butterflies—lying on a bed of heather at night, with a pale star or two glinting through the shelter of the branches.

Another day a couple came to the door asking for potatoes. From their accent I knew that they were French.

'Des pommes de terre. Je regrette...'

Amazement lit their faces. 'You speak French? Up here?'

I laughed. 'Oh, yes. We're quite civilized!'

We lapsed into good-humoured French. They were camping in the wood down near the bottom of the hill, they said. They had been there for several days and were running short of supplies. If there were no farms, was there, perhaps, a shop? I had to say sorry on both counts, then had them in to tea and ransacked the larder for something to keep them going. I filled a bag with oatmeal and a jar with honey and told them how to make brose.

'Just hot water stirred into the oatmeal? No cooking?'

'That's right. You get all the goodness, the vitamins and minerals and you can add anything you like—a little salt, honey, whisky! It'll keep you going all day!'

They laughed. 'That's wonderful!'

'It is. It's what has kept the Highland people fit and strong.'

'You don't grow oats, but you have bees?'

'Yes.'

'May we, perhaps, see them, another time?'

'Of course.'

We parted on friendly terms. I was sure they would be back. They were: many times over that summer they would appear, saying everything was fine, they had made a shelter in the wood, had a good fire for cooking and warmth, a pool in the burn for washing, in fact, they could stay happily there for ever. They knew how to live off the land, gathering wild raspberries, strawberries, blaeberries and fungi, guddling for trout, snaring rabbits. It was great, they said, to discard all the trappings of urban life and they were grateful that no one turned them away in disapproval. They offered to give me a hand with jobs about the garden, an offer I was glad to accept. There was never a hint of scrounging.

It turned out that he was from Corsica, had joined the Foreign Legion, as many young Corsicans did and was sent on some sort of mission to South America. There, he witnessed the inhumane treatment of the native peoples and was so revolted by it that he joined up with an Indian tribe and lived as one of them for a year. Did that mean he went A.W.O.L.? We never enquired.

One day he came up on his own, carrying a long, slender piece of wood.

'This is how the Indians hunt. I'll show you.'

He inserted something into the end of the wooden shaft, put the other end to his mouth and blew.

'Of course. A blow-pipe.'

'That's it. With a small poisoned arrow you can kill many kinds of game. You have to, when you're hungry!'

I drew back, hoping there was no poisoned arrow in this particular pipe. He smiled.

'Don't worry. There are no poisons here!'

Sadly, as autumn came and just when their wood was bearing a wonderful harvest of hazel-nuts, brambles, rose-hips and all kinds of fungi, they decided they would have to move. He had been making many beautiful things out of material he found to hand—wood, bone, stone—and had hoped to make a small income from selling them. Innately an artist, he never got round to the marketing side. Before moving on, he left us a gift—a most marvellously carved ceremonial machete, as made by the Indians he loved. I treasure it. I had lent him a copy of a book I had written about our life in the crofting community before we came to the schoolhouse. He said it would improve his English. As we said our goodbyes he asked: 'May I translate your book into French? I like it. May I?'

'Of course. That would be good.' And he did. We kept in touch and some months later the French version arrived. So far no French publisher has been found.

During the months that they were living in the wood their privacy was respected, no one intruded. Then, one day, after they had gone, a stray walker, taking a short cut up the hill, came on their encampment. An excited young man arrived at the door.

'What's going on down there, in the wood?' He was glaring at me, as though I were involved in something unspeakable.

'What do you mean?'

'You don't know? Look.'

He produced some instant photographs, holding them high for inspection. 'There's something very strange happening there. I don't know. It looks like witchcraft to me.'

'*Witchcraft*?'

I looked at the photographs. I had never been near their place, the Corsican's place, not wanting to intrude, but I realised these were pictures of their encampment. They had clearly left the branches of the shelter, knowing they would rot away naturally. In the bushes were some animal bones, the skull of a sheep he had found dead at the roadside, I remembered. These were the materials of his trade, his art. There was a pattern of stones beside the fireplace and an old iron pot full of water. An Indian tradition, I remembered he had told me, was to leave shelter, water and firing for whoever might pass by. Surely a Highland tradition, the tradition of hospitality. I smiled and tried to explain something of this to the excited young man. He was unconvinced.

'I think there's more to it than that. Have you heard of any practices of witchcraft in the neighbourhood?'

'I have not.'

'Well...I'm going to show these to someone who'll be interested. A journalist. He'll send a professional photographer out.'

'Please don't do that.'

'It'll make a good story.'

'An entirely false one.'

He named a paper which might be interested in the story, sufficiently to pursue it.

'May I use your phone?' He was determined to have his say.

'I'm sorry. I have some calls to make. There's a phone box up the road.' It was seldom we refused to help.

'Right. Cheers.'

Cheers? There were none from me! I spent the rest of the day making phone calls to the paper he mentioned, getting doubtful answers all along the line. Witchcraft? The word seemed to have irresistibly magic connotations. From people at various stages up the editorial ladder there were unsatisfactory responses, each one reluctant to let go of such an exciting item. At last I reached the editor himself, explaining that I had known the people involved personally, that a story of witchcraft would bring many unwelcome visitors, maybe even practitioners of the black arts, to the area, that the folk who lived here would naturally be upset and angry. Eventually, after a long conversation, he agreed that the 'story' should not be written up.

All this did not detract from the value of the legacy which visitors such as the loner in his shelter on the hill and the Corsicans in the wood left with us. They bought few stamps, letter-writing was not their business, though they sent a card home from time to time. But what they left could not be counted in monetary terms. It was rather a sense of perspective, of seeing oneself as part of the huge structure of rock and sky, of river and loch, woodland with its bright-eyed creatures, and moors with flowering moss. Living in this perspective meant working along with the natural forces, with wind and storm, along with the heat of the sun, the light of the stars, accepting them all as beneficent. Perhaps, with time and talent, things of surprising beauty can be made out of the natural things lying about, with the simplest of tools. We learnt this, too. I often look at the Indian-style machete, run my hand over the smooth wood, study the intricate design of the stones and the delicate, carved images of eagle and deer.

XX

The Post in the Islands

Latterly, when my husband had not been well, we rarely went away for a holiday. There was always the problem of finding a substitute postmaster and the upheaval was quite great. But after I had been working on my own for a time I thought a break would be a good idea and, to my great delight, a young neighbour was more than pleased to act as holiday relief. She had been a good customer herself and quickly picked up the idea of working from the other side of the counter. Knowing that things were in capable hands I could set off confidently for a couple of weeks. Inevitably, I made for the west and the islands of the west. On arrival in each island I went to over the years I would make for the post office and have an interesting discussion about procedures, problems and so on. In my first island, Barra, I found the office in Castlebay had its notice above the door in Gaelic. It was good to see the native language take precedence. It was run in conjunction with a shop and was a very busy place in the summer.

The first post office in Barra was established in 1855. As the average number of letters posted per week at that time was only 67, bringing in four pounds, ten shillings and fourpence, and the estimated cost of operating was £18 (£3 salary for the postmaster and £15 for the ferry to South Uist) the business was run at a loss. The first postmaster was Dr MacGilivray, who was also the medical doctor and factor for the estate. He lived in the mansion house at Eoligarry which had been built by the MacNeils. The newly established Fishery Company was pressing for a better postal service and in 1875 the office at Castlebay, where the steamers came in, was opened. The postmaster also acted as 'runner', delivering the mail on foot.

In later years Compton Mackenzie had a house on Barra. During the Second World War the postmaster had to transmit by Morse code a series of telegrams to Compton Mackenzie's publishers in London, postal services being often subject to delay. These turned out to be the outlines of his famous book *Whisky Galore*! Sailing packets kept the mails going between all the islands. Now, of course, Barra has its own special air-mail delivery, when the Post Bus meets the plane coming in to land on the famous cockle beach.

In Iona English was used in the name of the office. There was even a board announcing 'Telegraph Office' with an arrowed sign. There were no postal facilities on the island before the mid-nineteenth century. People had to make their own arrangements to collect their mail at Bunessan in Mull. In 1851 a runner was appointed to take letters to Fionnphort and thence across the sound to Iona by open-decked ferry boat. He did this for three shillings a week, out of which he had to pay sixpence as ferry charge. A small receiving office was set up in Iona.

As the tourist trade to Iona increased greatly during the nineteenth century special mail runs were made from Tobermory during the summer and there were extra deliveries from Bunessan, where mounted postmen had taken over from the runners. Many thousands of post-cards have been sent from Iona over the years, yet the same hand-stamp was used for nearly half a century. The postmaster —or mistress—today must have to answer many queries expressed in broken English regarding rates of postage to many parts of the world, as visitors from overseas eagerly throng the island. Day-trippers, too, want their cards date-stamped 'Iona' and have no time to queue as their steamer awaits. Much patience must be needed in that small office!

For centuries the islands have felt themselves to be isolated, their language, customs, whole way of life different from that of most parts of the mainland. By the eighteenth century, however, they were gradually being drawn into the web of the modern world. The clan chiefs had lost their status as fathers of the clans and were becoming landlords anxious to make their vast clan lands, their estates, pay dividends. The kelp industry—the burning of sea-weed to produce potash—was flourishing, there was development in the fishing business and large numbers of sheep were being imported to provide wool for the factories in the south. Later, there would be the letting of the shooting and fishing to wealthy patrons from all parts. All these developments demanded contacts with the mainland

The post office on the island of Coll (The Post Office)

and the only means of communication was by written message, that is, by the post. The native people wrote few letters, their language having a largely oral tradition. Writing things down was said to damage the memory! But the landlords—the Campbells, the Mackenzies, the Macdonalds, the Macleans, were all English-speaking and literate. They made their words heard! So desperate were they to get postal services established that they sometimes ran them at their own expense and even persuaded their tenants (as the clansmen had become) to take a share in the cost. They did take on the responsibility of providing guarantors should some schemes fail disastrously.

Another of my much-loved islands is Coll. In the principal village of Arinagour there is now a flourishing small post office, which also sells postcards, small booklets and other items of interest to visitors. In 1829 the landlords and tenants of Coll, along with those of Tiree, had to petition the Post Office to provide a regular, costed service by sailing packet. Hitherto they had had to provide it at their own expense. Freeling, the man at the top, regarded their request sympathetically and, as the amount of correspondence was estimated at only £15 a year, it was granted, experimentally, for twelve months. It was not successful, but was continued for a further year, on condition that the proprietors guaranteed revenue against loss. The distribution of letters within the island was another matter. There was no attempt to deliver mail locally for another fifty years, though by 1903 it was agreed that purely local mail could be delivered on days when the steamer failed to call, which could be quite often during the times of winter storms.

One drawback to the arrival of mail in Coll was the fact that large steamers could not anchor in the harbour and had to be unloaded off-shore and passengers, cargo and mail to be ferried ashore in a rowing-boat. Since then a great new pier has been built and there are now roll-on, roll-off facilities for motorists!

Raasay was an island I had for long wanted to visit. We had often heard and read about its owner, the famous Dr 'No', a medical man from the south of England who had steadfastly refused to allow a car-ferry from Sconser, on the neighbouring island of Skye, to operate. Iron ore had been discovered in 1896 and a Lanarkshire Company—Bairds—had built a railway line from the mine to the pier. The bed of this line can still be followed and makes a pleasant walk. During the First World War German prisoners had worked the mine. A mail-cart was used to convey letters and parcels, twice a week, from the post office to the pier. The presence of the prisoners had greatly increased the volume of mail. But the working of the mine was not a viable enterprise and the rusting machinery was eventually sold as scrap.

In the eighteenth century a ferry-boat operated weekly between Sconser and Raasay. It is reported that Dr Johnson, who stayed in the big house during his famous tour, wrote a letter to Boswell dated 10 April 1775 which only reached its recipient in London on 6 May. One wonders through how many hands and how many ferries and mail-bags it passed! A receiving office was established in Raasay in 1803, with a salary of £2 for the receiver. Later a sub-office was opened at Torran, in the north of the island, and a postal service extended over the strait to Rona, for the lighthouse there.

In 1904 Miss Mary Macmillan was postmistress in Raasay. Her predecessor and 'Deliverer', that is the person who delivered the letters, according to a memorandum dated 12 March 1907, are 'both in the employ of Mrs Wood [wife of the owner of the island], the Renter of the private bag, and although both are aware that they were entitled to payment, preferred to accept presents, usually at Christmas. Articles of clothing were given to the Deliverer, but he also received perquisites in the form of game, etc.' This is surely an example of the paternalism, or maternalism, prevailing at the time.

When old age pensions were introduced in 1909—at five shillings a week—the people on Rona got their money from the local post-man, who received a penny for every pension he paid out. He was a travelling post office! The office at Torran was closed at the start of the First World War and the mails for that area were delivered by a mounted postman from the south of the island. Rona, how-ever, could only be served by a foot-post. Mary Macleod, the 17-year-old daughter of the former postmaster at Torran, carried the mail-bag along a perilous coastal foot-path to the tidal island of Fladday.

The north of the island became famous for the work of John Macleod who, working with pick, shovel and barrow, hacked out a road to link his community with the south. I travelled this road and was entertained happily to tea in his house by his grandchildren. The post office in Raasay is now a busy and popular place, part of the general store in the village of Clachan.

Raasay, to me, meant, of course, Hallaig and the wonderful poem of that name by Sorley Maclean. I walked there, on a perfect sum-mer day. The sadness of the little ruined houses in their stretch of bright green sward was intense, but even over the desolation the beauty of the poem and the promise of it rose, like a shaft of light.

Eigg is another island, one of the many, which has suffered from absent landowners who have neglected it and used it as a plaything. As I write, it is at last enjoying the right to be itself, in the hands of dedicated Trustees. When I visited the post office was running as part of the one shop, in the middle of the island. It is such a little place, six miles long, four miles wide. On arrival by small ferry-boat from the big steamer I found I had missed any kind of transport to anywhere. I found a phone, booked myself into a farmhouse and walked there happily on a traffic-free road.

It was in 1874 that a post and telegraph office was opened on the island. In 1897 a foot-post to Cleadale, in the north-west, was instituted and, later, another to the south coast. A weekly ferry by sailing-boat to the small island of Muck took mail for the people there, who had no post office of their own. The steamer from Green-ock to Stornoway delivered mail twice a week in summer and once in winter, which had to be trans-shipped by rowing-boat to the landing quay. On her way south the steamer called again, the post-master at Portree telegraphing the sub-postmaster in Eigg to tell him the time of departure from Skye, so that the boatman at Eigg could be standing by. This was to prevent undue delay in MacBrayne's schedule.

MacBrayne's certainly ruled the waves round the Western Isles then, as they do today. I wonder who composed this scurrilous, well-known verse:

> The earth belongs unto the Lord
> And all that it contains
> Except the Western Islands, they
> Belong unto MacBraynes.
> *(To be sung in the manner of a metrical Psalm)*

Today, of course, the isolation of the islands is very much less than it was. Occupation by the land and air forces, use of the deep waters by submariners, all these developments, still much in evidence in spite of the ending of the Cold War, have meant a vast proliferation of facilities for rapid communication with the centres of power. The native people benefit from these facilities to a certain extent, but the change in tempo does not suit them all. There are signs of reaction which bode well, I think, for a healthy readjustment between old and new.

In Gigha—God's island—I stayed in the actual post office. It's part of the busy shop in the village of Ardminish. This shop is on the ground floor of a substantial house which was at one time the school and the schoolmaster's residence. On the upper floor are rooms let to summer visitors. A motor launch from Tayinloan serves the island. A receiving house was first established in 1859. After many ups and downs in the establishment of house-to-house delivery of mail, with interceptions by landowners and M.P.s, order now reigns. The problem in Gigha, as in so many of the islands, was the small number of letters posted, the revenue in postage not meeting the cost of running the service. Today, with increasing numbers of visitors and some stabilising of resident populations, the losses are less.

Another island which I had visited briefly once before and which I had long hoped to see again, was Lismore. It is so easy of access—

ten minutes in a ferry-boat from Port Appin. In older times the ferry was summoned by a blast on the horn. St Moluag founded a monastery on Lismore, which eventually housed the cathedral of Argyll and the Isles. Many famous clerics served the parish. In the *New Statistical Account* of 1841 the Reverend Gregor MacGregor says:

> There is a great improvement in the Post Office since the old statistical account...at that time the mail came only three times a week from Inverary: but now there is a daily post contributing greatly to the improvement of the parish: and there is a penny post at Lismore, to which there is a runner twice a week from Appin...so easy and expeditious is now the communication with the south that a newspaper that is published in Glasgow in the morning is in Appin that night and may be, and often is, in Lismore next morning.

A post office had been established in Appin as early as 1788 and by 1831 an onward delivery to Lismore was in operation, with a receiving house at the northern end of the island, which was later removed to Clachan. One Lismore family, the MacColls, served the posts through Lismore for six generations. Today the post office is situated in a shop at a central spot, convenient for people from all parts of the island. Protests and petitions and interventions by clerics and M.P.s have meant that the receipt and delivery of the mail by ferry and van is adequate. And there is a Post Bus on which I travelled happily on several occasions.

Colonsay I visited during that week in June 1995 when the temperature rose to unbelievable, hitherto unrecorded, heights. The post office is in a well-stocked store near the landing-stage. A friendly postman runs the post bus on which passengers can take the slightly hair-raising passage across the tidal sands to Oronsay. Lord Colonsay—Duncan MacNeil, the lawyer—managed to get a postal service for the island in 1871, with a receiving office at Scalasaig and a twice-weekly service to other parts. There were the usual problems with the cost of the service proving uneconomic and vicissitudes in the provision of steamer sailings. But eventually things evened out, communication being vastly improved by the introduction of telegraph cables and, later, telephone links. While glad to remain isolated as a retreat from the hurly-burly of life on the mainland, Colonsay is nevertheless happily confident that contact can be established at will. The need for this is especially great today as a publishing house, dealing largely with Scottish books, has been established and is run in conjunction with an excellent bookshop at the hotel.

An unusual way of improving communication with some of the islands was tried out in 1934 with a possible link between Harris and the small island of Scarp—by rocket. Gerhard Zucker, a German inventor, whose speciality was rocket propulsion, had the idea of firing mail-carrying rockets from the island to Harris. Sadly, this was not a success. The rocket exploded on detonation and the letters were scattered far and wide. Some were salvaged, charred or scorched. Zucker was later involved in war-time rocket experiments in Germany.

XXI
Electronic Mail

On arrival home from one of my islands I always feel a renewed sense of solidarity with all the servants of the Post Office. Those I have met on my travels have all taught me something. Observing their ways, comparing notes, listening to their experiences and problems is an inspiration for work in one's own sphere...

In many ways our own small place, though it is only ten miles from the capital of the Highlands, has less contact with the wider world than some of those in the off-shore islands—Iona with its thousands of visitors, Benbecula with its army of occupation and its busy airfield. Soon, however, it was to take itself onto the modern map, with the arrival of the new technology.

On a walk up the road one autumn afternoon I found a large white van drawn into a lay-by and two men delving into the ground. The van door was open. Glancing inside, I saw the most marvellous collection of multi-coloured wires coiled in a dazzling pattern.

'Looks like the end of the rainbow!' I said, in amazement.

They smiled. 'Aye. I don't know if it's the end. Maybe it's just the beginning.'

As they worked away, smoothing out the wires, putting them in place, they explained that this was part of a vast plan for linking the Highlands with the world-wide network of communication. Network? Web? Internet? Where had I heard those words? I looked up at the sky. It was pale green as the light was fading. There was a streak of rose-red at the horizon.

'You mean...all these messages are coming through the air. And what are they telling us?' I was talking to myself, really, but the men were happy to make it a conversation.

'Aye. I sometimes wonder about that. The telly's enough for me. And there's good stuff on the radio. But what's in those wires, that doesn't bother me.'

The other man laughed. 'I get plenty blether from the wife. And I like time to think a bit, too.'

Were these two kindred spirits? I watched them working away with such precision, deftly, the coloured wires passing smooth and straight through their hands. It was clear they knew exactly what they were doing. They were part of this great conglomeration, this great structure, should I say, of the world of information technology, yet they were still human, apart, not overwhelmed. Information? About what? Did I want to know exactly what the price of sugar shares was that day, who was likely to start an offensive in the troubles in Indonesia? Surely these things are of great importance to some people, but, having got the answer you were, perhaps, looking for, would there not be a temptation to go on pressing buttons, turning switches, quizzing the ether, till you found yourself engulfed in a mass of facts and figures impossible to digest? I remembered those flickering screens I'd seen in shop windows. Headaches and eye-strain must afflict the devotees, I thought.

I said goodbye to the engineers and walked on. The information I was seeking was the whereabouts of the wild swans on the loch up the road. They had just arrived. Were they in the rushes on the far bank or near the outlet which was hidden by the trees? My own two eyes would give me the answer.

Since that day and the coming of the magic wires, 'tele-cottages' have arrived in the area. Their operators patronise the post office, buying quite large quantities of stamps, sending off packets and so on. This is, of course, very welcome. The whole idea of doing office-type work from home is a good one. It cuts down on the use of cars, those perpetrators of the sin against the ozone layer. It allows time for the development of small subsidiary enterprises, such as organic gardening and the tending of livestock, so keeping a small acreage in production and making for a balanced life-style, with the flow of 'information' kept in check.

Our 'tele-cottages' are Aladdin's caves, full of wonders. Wires, screens, recorders, computers, word-processors, shine from every corner. But the two with which I'm familiar boast, also, I'm glad to say, bevies of chickens in the garden ground, one has a few sheep scavenging the hens' food, another keeps bees and ducks.

There will never be an end, of course, to the inventiveness of people everywhere and to the general speeding-up of every process of manufacture, transportation, communication. We are now in the era of electronic mail. This service can only be used by those who have the necessary devices for the transmission and reception of the messages. As a means of keeping in touch, at short notice, with friends or relatives in far-off parts of the world it is greatly valued by those who have the equipment. As private individuals they must be few in number.

I think back, again, to the bundles of letters from my daughter and grand-daughter, kept tucked away and re-read for the feel of youth and energy they contain and for the elegance of the handwriting. Is the time for the writing of letters slipping away altogether? When I look at some of the scribbles of the very young and the odd spellings...I wonder. The stationers' shops are full of attractive packages of letter-writing equipment—coloured or decorated paper and envelopes, pens of all kinds—even the old fountain pen coming back into circulation. These make quite acceptable presents at Christmas-time, but are mostly, I suspect, put away at the back of a drawer, or passed on, unopened, to an unsuspecting relative or friend.

What about the production of books, I often wonder. Students still wander around with two or three under their arm. The library has a queue of readers waiting to check books in or out. At the occasional charity book sale scores of buyers hunt for bargains, and find them. Hard-backs £1, paper-backs 50p. In discarding the rubbish, treasures can be found. People must be reading.

Could we, perhaps, tire of the race to be first with the news? What news? The newness of events all over the world? I remember our tele-cottages when they were croft houses, places where you went visiting on a winter evening when work for the day was done. You would smell the peat reek as you came near the door and would know there was a good fire on. You'd enter, pushing the door, without knocking. Through the pipe smoke friendly eyes would peer from behind the pages of the newspaper. No virtual reality here, but a cup of tea, or a dram, then some drastic criticism of the Government's many failures—a Government that can't even control the weather!—maybe a tune on the accordion if the mood was swinging that way, and home again, warmed and cheered.

The tele people in occupation now have swept away all the

cobwebs, letting in light and air. There's not a warm, dusky corner to be found. Muddy boots must be left at the door. Should we, we wonder, perhaps have a shower before coming in? They are good people, I'm sure, but it's difficult to make real contact when they seem to spend so much of their time on the telephone, even when they're feeding the hens outside, or transfixed by the dazzle of the messages they've called up, or scrutinising the words as they appear on the computer screen. When, one wonders, do they switch everything off and relax?

Highland people have for long been accustomed to welcoming the stranger in their midst. We knew this when we first arrived and found ready help to erect a larch pole with a small engine and rotary blades attached which was to make electricity to light the house. The neighbours must have thought it was a pretty daft idea, but their code of manners would never let them say so and they were generously happy when they found it did work. So the tele people will, I'm sure, find their place as they settle down with all their magic wires in place. Maybe we shall manage, in time, to learn enough of the new language of technology to be able to carry on a discussion on the merits of the new communication systems.

One thing I think I shall never accept is the electronic pet. What's wrong with a good old moggy if you haven't time to walk a dog? She'll keep down the mice which might chew your cabling to shreds in the winter cold. You can stroke her and listen to her purr and she'll warm your chair on a chilly evening. There must be something beyond the surfing of the web. What about those glorious beaches on the island of Tiree?

XXII
From Bishop Mark to
Postmark

We had always been proud of the fact that our office had its own hand-stamper, brass with a wooden handle, clearly marked with its own name along with the date. Most other small offices came under the umbrella of Inverness. Quite often we would receive a request from a collector of postmarks to date-stamp a couple of stamped envelopes he enclosed. We were happy to oblige.

In the early days of stamp-collecting it was considered best to have new specimens in mint condition in one's collection. Latterly, clearly postmarked stamps, still adhering to the paper, were preferred. The postmark as we know it today, a circular mark on the envelope, obliterating the postage stamp and showing clearly the name of the office where it was posted and the date of posting, this postmark owes its origin to the fact that, in England, in the seventeenth century, there were many complaints about delays in the delivery of letters. Often, on an urgent letter, people would write the words 'Haste, post, haste!' with a little sketch of a gallows with a post-boy hanging. The addresses were often extremely imprecise. For instance, an Ebenezer Halcrow might be addressed as 'living near the bridge' with the name of the town or village added.

There was a complaint that mail-bags going from London to Edinburgh were being opened on the way, on the excuse that they were not properly labelled. Colonel Henry Bishop, who was running the Post Office at the time, ordered that, to prevent this 'breaking open the Scotch Baggs' every bag was to be securely sealed with a brass tag, each postmaster who handled it to certify that the seal was unbroken. As complaints about the delays continued Bishop declared that 'a stamp is invented that is putt upon every letter shewing the day of the moneth that every letter comes to the office, so that no Letter Carryer may dare detayne a letter from post to post, which before was usual.' These marks were known as Bishop marks and their use continued, with certain changes in size and shape, until the early nineteenth century.

In the days of the mail-coach, in the eighteenth century, the postmarks showed a figure representing the number of miles between the destination of the letter and London. This was a help for postmasters in calculating the postage charge which then depended on the distance travelled. Thus the mileage mark for Dumfries was the number 341, inscribed in a box below the name of the town.

After the introduction of the adhesive stamp the type of postmark which we know today came into use—this to prevent the re-use of the stamp. One type of postmark was known as the 'killer' as it totally obliterated the stamp.

A strange story concerning postmarks is that of their importance in the trial for murder of Madeleine Smith, in Glasgow, in 1857. Charged with the murder by arsenical poisoning of her lover Emile L'Angelier, proof of her guilt was dependent on the postmark of a letter sent by her to L'Angelier in which she referred to a meeting, after which he became ill. The postmark had been struck carelessly and was illegible. The controller of the sorting office in Glasgow, called to give evidence, admitted that he found the mark difficult to decipher. Addressing the jury the judge said: 'I trust that this will be the last occasion on which the postmarks are so carelessly impressed as they have been. It is a very important matter for the ends of civil and criminal justice that the postmark should be properly stamped.' So, for lack of evidence, the verdict was Not Proven, by a majority. This sensational trial and its outcome is still a matter for discussion. Madeleine Smith married twice and lived out a long life in America. The Glasgow postmarks of the time were withdrawn soon after the end of the trial. To the lucky philatelist who possesses a few of them they are known as 'the Madeleine Smiths.' The moral of this story, for all postmasters, is surely—'Watch your date-stamp, keep it cleaned and use it carefully.' I try to do this, but fail quite often, I admit.

The slogan postmark is one we know well today. It was another of Colonel Bishop's innovations back in the late seventeenth century. Eager to promote the use of the official postal services and to outdo rivals who were causing loss of revenue, he advertised the daily posts to the south with a slogan 'the post for all Kent goes every night from the Round House in Love Lane and comes every morning'. The practice then lapsed for two and a half centuries till, during the First World War, the Post Office introduced a slogan— 'Buy National War Bonds'. As a publicity measure the imposing of slogans was soon seen to be important. 'Post early in the day', 'Say it by telephone' were used during World War Two. 'Dig for Victory' was a winner. The 'Empire exhibition Glasgow May-October 1938' was the first specifically Scottish postmark. It had a lion rampant incorporated in the design.

After 1956 the G.P.O. allowed postmarks to be used, not only for Government-sponsored campaigns, but to mark anniversaries or events of a more local type. For instance 'National Bible Society of Scotland 1809-1959'. Later, tourist publicity was allowed. 'Inverness the Highland Capital' was used between 1963 and 1965. The use of postmarks as an inexpensive form of publicity gradually became widespread. The proliferation of so many divers types has created a wide field for collectors to explore. Most have had to restrict themselves to amassing those of a certain type, or relating to a certain theme or location. Most often the slogan is cut from the envelope, with the date-stamp and the postage stamp intact. Sometimes the whole envelope is collected.

Today we take slogans on envelopes so much for granted that we tend to ignore them. In front of me, as I write, I have an attractive example—'Scottish Wildlife Trust' in capital letters, 'Working for wildlife' in script and a pattern of lines in an oval frame. Alongside is the Edinburgh date-stamp, very clearly registered and the postage paid. This is a first-class example, clear and uncluttered, which could well grace a collector's album.

XXIII
Travelling Post Offices

Often, in my young days, when it was great adventure to have a 'pen-pal', especially one who lived in a far-off country, I used to wonder how this fragile piece of paper, with my name inscribed on it, had reached me safely across the miles of mountain and sea. I would scan the postmark and the date of posting and marvel again at the speed of its delivery. The stamps, too, were a joy, most often of Canadian origin, for there were relatives there and I was an avid reader of Jack London. Later, I was to have correspondence with people in many places—Europe and the Far East—and it was always a thrill to read their letters. The handwriting, even the paper, was different, inviting, calling up a picture of the writer. Thoughts and feelings, accounts of activities, descriptions of place, all these things, even clumsily expressed, if read with sympathetic understanding, do make for a real sense of communication. Letter-writing is going out now, I know. Attractive 'notelets' tempt one to write only short notes. Everything speeds on, regardless.

The postal authorities have always been aware of the need for speed, since the days of the post-boys who could be deported for 'dallying'. In the mid-nineteenth century, the heyday of Victorian Britain, when everything was on the move, including the railways, the Post Office, feeling 'bound to keep pace with the wonderful improvements with which the present age abounds', decided to make use of this latest form of transport.

The first bags of mail were taken over from the coaches, sometimes including the coaches themselves and the guard. There were fears for the safety of the mail on the first railroads in England. The track had to be lit the whole way at night. One Superintendent of Mail Coaches reported to London, 'Conceive an engine and five or six large carriages in its train rushing along at 20 miles an hour...the

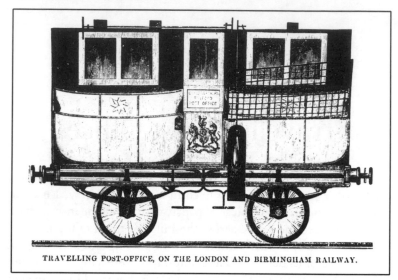

TRAVELLING POST-OFFICE, ON THE LONDON AND BIRMINGHAM RAILWAY.

The first Travelling Post Office, put into service in 1838 (The Post Office)

constant care of the Road Engineers may prevent all accident but it has a frightful appearance.'

In order to speed the mail even further, in 1838 the first Travelling Post Office, a converted horse-box, was put into service. It was a great success as it made possible the sorting and exchange of mail en route. As in the days of the mail coaches the mail-bags could be thrown out at certain points, as the train slowed, and the in-coming bag could be taken on board by means of a pole stretched towards a worker in the office.

Working conditions in the early Travelling Post Offices were atrocious. The carriages were fitted with counters, desks and pigeon-holes, but there was poor ventilation and no seating or sanitary provision. Many workers travelled as many as forty nights consecutively in order to make up their pitiful allowance. Between 1860 and 1867 there were 28 accidents in which post office men were killed or badly injured. Fumes given out by the oil lamps and the wax used for sealing the bags caused nausea and even affected the brain. Some workers were forced to retire at an early age, even in their mid-thirties, with paralysis or mental debility. Slowly, conditions improved. The railway network was spreading fast. In June 1862 an express train left King's Cross station in London at 10 a.m.

every morning bound for the Waverley station in Edinburgh, 393 miles away. This was the *Flying Scotsman*. As the main-line railways reached Scotland, the railway post offices soon followed, the first, the *Caledonian*, running from Carlisle to Glasgow in 1848.

An outstanding example of Post Office efficiency occurred in the aftermath of the Tay Bridge disaster of Sunday 28 December 1879. The bridge carried the main railway line from Edinburgh to Aberdeen. As a north-bound slow train, carrying 6 bags of mail and 78 passengers, approached the bridge in the evening a gale of alarming ferocity was blowing. The train proceeded but the centre section of the bridge collapsed. The whole train and all the people on it disappeared into the waters of the Tay.

That same evening two mail bags were recovered from the beach at Broughty Ferry, four miles downstream. The letters were sent to Dundee and dried out. They were delivered the next day. Only seven of the recovered letters have been traced.

In 1885 came the first of the special Mail Trains which were not intended to carry passengers and were used only for the work of the Post Office. With the ever-increasing volume of mail, particularly business items, newspapers and Government circulars as well as personal letters, this was a necessary move. Soon fifty men were working in about a dozen coaches. Crewe became the 'night mail capital of the United Kingdom'. The Night Mail train stirred the emotions of the people as the old mail coaches had done many years before. W.H.Auden caught the mood of the time in a wonderful poem he wrote as part of the commentary to the film *Night Mail* which John Grierson produced in 1936 for the G.P.O. Film Unit. In it you can hear all the nostalgia of the railway age, as well as the sound and rhythm of the train. It's so good I can't resist quoting its opening lines:

> This is the night mail crossing the border,
> Bringing the cheque and the postal order,
> Letters for the rich, letters for the poor,
> The shop at the corner and the girl next door.
> Pulling up Beattock, a steady climb—
> The gradient's against her but she's on time.

XXIV
The Post at Sea

Those letters I used to get from relatives and 'pen-pals' in Canada and Australia and elsewhere had travelled, I realised, at least half the way from their place of origin, not overland, but over the water. Throughout the years, messages, despatches, letters of love must all have been moving over calm waters, through storm and shipwreck, attack by pirates and enemies, through days and nights many times more perilous than those passed on land. Being an island has great advantages—no fear of invasion by land, perhaps, but there are drawbacks. In the days before the conquest of the air there was the sea in constant contention.

In England, as far back as the reign of Henry VIII, a vessel carrying despatches ran from Dover to the continent. Aptly named the *Post Horse*, it was a small sailing ship with a crew of six to eight and could carry a dozen passengers. These vessels were known as Packet Boats or Packets. Hence the French word *Paquebot*.

During the ups and downs of the relationship with Ireland in the sixteenth and seventeenth centuries it was essential to keep a postal service going across the North Channel for military as well as commercial purposes. Queen Anne's Act of 1711 combined the English and Scottish Post Offices and a regular service of packet boats to Ireland was established.

This packet service was greatly extended over the years. The vessels, built for speed rather than security and unarmed except in time of war, flew a special flag as identification—the 'Post-boy Jack', showing a rider blowing a post-horn. During the Napoleonic wars the packet boats encountered many dangers. The working conditions were appalling and the pay poor yet the crews performed amazing acts of bravery in the protection of the Royal Mail, fighting off French pirates and, in one case, actually boarding and capturing a privateer.

The Falmouth Packet, 1822 (The Post Office)

After a small quantity of tea and tobacco was smuggled ashore and seized by the Customs at Falmouth in 1810 the packet men mutinied, demanding better pay. The Riot Act was read and thereafter the Admiralty took control of the packet stations.

Without the stimulus of military necessity, as in the case of Ireland, postal services for the Scottish islands lagged far behind those for other overseas destinations. However, soon after the Rebellion of 1745, a link between Lewis and the mainland was organised, mainly through the enterprise of local lairds and merchants. There were many hazards—bad weather, long distances and poor roads, as well as the obstinacy and parsimony of the postal officials in London, who had no idea of the conditions prevailing in the Islands and often paid little heed to the reports of their Surveyors. The Islands, as well as the mainland area of the Highlands, were awakening to the possibilities of trade, particularly in the fishing industry, the manufacture of seaweed products and so on and were no longer to be looked on as wild and remote. So, at last, it was agreed that a sailing packet would take mail from Stornoway to Poolewe whence it could go by foot-post to Dingwall and thence to Inverness. The Post Office made a contribution to the cost of the service, but the Earl of Seaforth, proprietor of Lewis, paid most of the balance.

The difficulties encountered by the letter-carriers of the time are graphically described in a memorandum sent to the Postmaster General for Scotland in 1798 by Lord Macdonald, Macleod of Macleod, Clanranald and other landowners in Skye and the Uists:

> The Posts from Dunvegan to Inverness, who go alternately, week about have an allowance each of 5s. for every time they go to Inverness, a journey going and returning of fully 226 miles including six ferries. This sum of 5s., it is evident, cannot be an inducement for any man to take such a journey and the Post of necessity has been and is still the Carrier for the whole country, and from being overloaded with commissions he very frequently is detained beyond his usual time, and he generally takes a small boat at loch Carron whereby his own life as well as the mail is in imminent danger of being lost.

Just as roads were being made and improved in the early nineteenth century, so waterways were also being developed. The Crinal Canal in 1801 and the Caledonian Canal 22 years later allowed traffic to pass from Glasgow to Inverness. Small paddle steamers were plying along the west coast and by 1851 the famous red and black funnels of MacBraynes's steamships were to be seen. Two of the best-known steamers were the *Columba* and the *Iona*, on which the Post Office installed travelling post offices.

For letters to Orkney and Shetland the Post Office agreed, after much persuasion, to make a payment of twopence for each item to the captain of the vessel carrying them. They were known as 'ship letters'. This amount was charged over and above the normal postage. Such a system of payment to the captains of ships was used by the Post Office for the world-wide transport of mails.

In the early 1800s steam was being developed as a great source of power. It could provide energy to drive engines to pull trains on land and energy to move paddles to progress the movement of ships on the water. So the great challenge arose—the crossing of the wide gulf of the Atlantic to foster communication with the increasing number of immigrants to America and with the enterprises that were developing there.

In April 1838 the Great Sea Race took place, the contestants being the *Great Western*, a ship designed by Brunel, and the *Sirius*, both carrying passengers and mail. The *Sirius* made the crossing from Cork in 18 days, and at the end had just 20 tons of coal left in her bunkers. The *Great Western* steamed into New York four days later, to be greeted by crowds of excited New Yorkers, having made the crossing in 15 days. Samuel Cunard, a ship-owner from Nova Scotia, was one of the first to realise the potential of steamship communication across the Atlantic. With ever-decreasing times for the voyage and several competing companies engaged in the business, the famous Blue Riband was awarded for record-breaking Atlantic crossings.

Mail services to India, Australia, New Zealand and South Africa, all parts of the world where British people were settled, had many problems to contend with. Conveyance, combined with overland carriage, was a long and cumbersome business. The invention of the screw propellor, which ousted the old paddle wheels, did help to make these long voyages feasible. In 1858 the Marine Mail Service set up sorting offices on the steam packets in order to accelerate the delivery of letters once port was reached. The sorters were obliged to provide themselves, at their own expense, with a distinctive uniform—a blue frock coat with Post Office buttons, dark 'pepper and salt' trousers and a forage cap with a gold band.

Later, a Sea Post Office, staffed jointly by British and American Post Office sorters, was set up. The ill-fated *Titanic* carried five such sorters, two British and three American, when she set off from Southampton on her maiden voyage in April 1912. The obituary of the sorters recorded how 'all five completely disregarded their own safety when the vessel sank, and began to carry the 200 sacks of the registered mail to the upper deck...As the situation became more desperate they appealed to the stewards to help them and continued their work to the last'. The vain attempt to save the Royal Mail showed the same spirit of dedicated service as that of the crews who fought the privateers a century earlier.

The deliverers of mail today do not have privateers or highwaymen to contend with, but they have problems of different kinds and they cope with them in the same spirit. Motorised vehicles don't mean the end of all troubles on the road. With black ice on the hill it's safer to sling a bag on your back and let your legs carry you and the mail. Our postie arrived one winter morning having survived a minor crash on the main road, his vehicle still usable but his head with a nasty bruise. 'Ach, it's nothing. I'll see the doctor later. Maybe.' It turned out he had a crack on the skull bone, but that only meant a couple of days' rest and he was back on the job.

XXV
Keeping in Touch against the Odds

My earliest non-contact with the Post Office service was when, in the early stages of the Second World War, I decided against applying for a job in the Censorship Office, which was based in Inverness. The idea of living and working in the Highlands was certainly a most attractive one, but the thought of reading letters from stranger to stranger, endlessly, day after day, looking for possible indiscretions regarding the war effort, or hints that might lower morale, was not appealing. There were many 'prohibited areas' in the Highlands during the war, as people planning holidays knew only too well. Training areas for the troops, deep-water anchorages for convoys, these and many other war-time 'facilities' were situated in the far north. Today these places are still looked on as 'facilities', that is, possible dumping-places for the waste products of the modern age.

In any war discretion is, of course, vital. Hence the 'secret service'. In peace-time, too, the utmost care must be taken in the dissemination of news of national importance. Hence the 'diplomatic bag'. In the Censorship Office, during the two world wars, letters from sensitive areas were officially opened and read, anything considered dangerous obliterated, and they were then resealed and marked. One of the earliest examples of censorship is that used during the Jacobite rebellion of 1745-46, when letters from Edinburgh to London were intercepted by the Highlanders, marked 'opened by the Rebels', then sent on to their destination.

In war-time the postal authorities had to adapt to many different situations. During World War Two various issues of stamps had to be made for the use of governments in exile in Britain. Poland, Yugoslavia, Holland and Norway issued stamps for use in the

117

*Cover of a letter sent during the 1745 uprising, marked 'open by the Rebells'
after being intercepted by the Highlanders*

army camps, these stamps often being used in the countries concerned after liberation.

Wars inevitably bring disturbances of kinds other than the actual fighting. Prisoners-of-war in their thousands are kept in camps.
Civilians are interned. For all these people some form of communication with the outside world has to be provided, on humanitarian
grounds. The Red Cross issued forms which the 'displaced' could
fill up to let their families know that they were alive, without giving away any information as to where they were, or indeed any
other factual matter.

For soldiers on active service contact with home is an essential
factor in keeping up morale. The transmission of letters to and
from the field appears incredibly difficult. Yet it was accomplished.
The numbers involved were enormous. There was also the prob-
lem of the movement of troops from one field of battle to another.
And the movements had to be kept secret. During the First World
War the British army operated a mail train, manned by the Royal
Engineers, for the delivery of letters. Servicemen could also post
letters on board and special postmarks were used—F.P.O., Field
Post Office.

The transmission of military orders and information required,
of course, the utmost secrecy. Speed was always essential. At one

time relays of skilled horsemen carried despatches hidden on their person, sometimes committed to memory. In later days despatch riders used motor-cycles, risking their lives on every journey.

During the Boer War Baden-Powell, who later founded the Boy Scout movement, organized scouts to undertake liaison work during the siege of Mafeking. A postal service was established, with stamps depicting a scout with a haversack, on his bicycle. During the Second World War, in Poland, boy scouts were involved in carrying mail, in secrecy, at great personal risk.

Postal authorities have had to deal with many contingencies other than war. Before the use of vaccines serious epidemics ravaged many countries. Plague, leprosy, smallpox, cholera and other diseases broke out, causing millions of deaths. As these diseases were highly infectious and more or less incurable, all that could be done was to protect towns by isolating them. Ships carrying infected passengers were to remain offshore, usually for a period of eighty days. Travellers reaching ports were to remain in quarantine, confined in special quarters, which were then fumigated. Goods were to be exposed to the air and ships treated with lime. Letters were considered high risk carriers of infection. They were fumigated at the quarantine stations and sometimes were specially postmarked. They could be split 'to let out the pestilential air', held over a sulphurous flame or sprinkled with vinegar, which was considered a disinfectant. Letters bearing the marks of these forms of purification can still be found. Vehicles carrying mail were equipped with sulphurous sprays to disinfect the boxes where letters were left.

Another emergency with which the postal authorities have to deal is industrial action by postal workers. Three times in quick succession—1962, 1964 and 1971—there were delays and breakdowns in the service in Britain. In 1962 the letter-mail was held up, but only for a few days. On this occasion the People's League for the Defence of Freedom organized a temporary service, until they were ordered to desist by the Post Master General as their effort constituted an infringement of Government monopoly. In 1964 the dispute amounted only to a 'go-slow', though some chaos ensued. In 1971, when a lengthy struggle was anticipated, the authorities, as we have seen, waived the Post Office monopoly, allowing many services to take over the work of handling the mail.

119

Before the coming of the railway, the carrying of mail posed problems enough in this country, with the hazards already described encountered by 'runners', post-boys and the mail-coach men. In other parts of the world the problems were greater and the means of overcoming them were ingenious in the extreme. Postal authorities everywhere have recognised the need that people have to communicate and also that that need is greatest in the most isolated areas. The more I learn about the measures taken to ensure that communication was maintained the more I marvel at the enterprise of the authorities concerned and at the courage and endurance of those who carried out the feats of daring which made a reality of the enterprise.

In North America there were deserts, unfriendly native tribes and high mountains to be encountered. The Pony Express company, subsequently part of 'Wells Fargo', operated a route with 600 hardy ponies, staging posts and, if needed, a small escort of cavalry. The isolated trading posts in Canada and Alaska communicated with the outside world by means of sledges drawn by dogs or reindeer.

Along the roads in the flat country of northern France and Belgium dogs were also used to pull small, two-wheeled mail carts. In the Nordic countries, where snow lies for months, the postmen travelled on skis. They were the cross-country skiers of their time and covered enormous distances. In remote mountainous country, where no motorised vehicle can venture, a sure-footed ass or a mule is still used to carry mail. In the marshy districts of south-west France, where stilts are commonly used for getting around, the postmen walked this way, covering the ground in great strides, the recipients of letters having to tread warily and stretch long arms to reach their mail.

It's clear that, since the earliest times, people the world over have had this strong desire to keep in touch and that organisations have been created to meet this desire, overcoming what seemed insuperable difficulties all along the line. Now, with air-mail, e-mail, fax machines, telecommunications of all kinds, it would seem that the problems are vanishing 'into thin air'. But are they, perhaps, only beginning, the problems? Are we casting aside the reality of a piece of paper, held in the hand, the texture felt, the individuality of the writing clearly recognised, are we casting this aside in favour of a few words on a crackling line, a flickering image, perhaps, on a dimly-lit screen, words on a long scroll turned out by a machine? Will all this dependence on mechanical devices not inhibit the true transmission of ideas and feelings which can really only be faithfully expressed in the intimate contact of pen with paper, made in quietness of mind? Will our correspondents become akin to all the other figures we see daily on our television screens, figures of virtual reality? There is still nothing comparable to the pleasure of receiving an envelope straight from the postman's hand, recognising the handwriting, admiring the stamp, slitting the seal, unfolding the paper and reading the lines.

The look of the handwriting is a joy in itself. The long loops, the leaning uprights, the rounded vowels, the scratchy middle consonants, the whole aspect of the sheet brings the writer to life. A science has evolved from the study of handwriting. I don't need that to help me identify the character of my friends. I love the spidery scrawl of the busy, lively minds, the more graceful, easy flow of the warm-hearted. I can still visualise my father's style, his slightly withdrawn, cramped script, with Greek 'e's and no flourishes. My mother's had a more rounded, less ethereal feel. They both wrote a lot but never used a typewriter.

Formal script can be learnt and has a beauty of its own, but I truly appreciate the individual quirks and talent of my letter-writers. Long may they fill the postie's bag and let the junk-mail be discarded on the internet!

XXVI
Problems with Parcels

We do not often have parcels to despatch from our office. The cost has risen alarmingly lately, making tokens an easier option to send as gifts. Nevertheless, in the weeks before Christmas we do have busy times, with the old scales and weights brought into operation, much looking-up of unfamiliar destinations and the postal rates thereto, the filling-up of Customs declarations, certificates of posting, checking information on insurance costs and rates of compensation in case of loss. This, we realise, is the kind of work done on a daily basis in the bigger offices. We are quite glad to be stretched in this way from time to time. It brings home to us, too, the fact that the postal services in some other countries are perhaps less strictly supervised than ours. When sending mail to one central European country I was advised not to put on attractive pictorial stamps as these were very often detached by collectors and the letter or packet remained undelivered as unstamped. Parcels to this particular country also most often disappeared en route.

These busy times bring people to our door who normally do their postal business in the town to which they commute daily. With us they dodge the queues. 'We must do this more often!' they say, as they heap their parcels on to every available space, ready for the postie to load them into his van in the morning. 'Why not?' we reply, thinking that such a volume of mail might justify an increase in our meagre pay!

The establishment of a Parcel Post lagged far behind that of the Government-controlled letter post. A reduced rate had been introduced for the sending of books through the letter-post, a special Book Post, which continued for many years. By the mid-1800s the railway companies had cornered most of the parcel business, though in the country districts carriers operated, with horse-drawn carts. These are remembered still, with affection, in many places.

After years of thoughtful discussion, research, visits abroad to inspect other ways of delivering parcels, the working out of practical details such as the building of depots and other problems in the actual handling of the goods, eventually, in August 1883, the Post Office was authorised to introduce the Parcel Post. Problems were soon encountered. Circulars were rushed out to postmasters everywhere. Damage to parcels due to insecure packing was a headache. One circular stated: 'Damage is occasioned to Parcels by the insecure packing of fruit. As a rule, fruit and butter should be sent in tins, even rather than in wooden boxes, as fruit (strawberries, raspberries, etc.) is reduced to a pulp by jolting in the trains and then exudes from the cracks of the Boxes.'

This reminds me of one instance when an untidy package, inadequately addressed, arrived in the post office at New Year time. The postie delivered it to what he took to be the right place. Two days later it reappeared with us. It was a case of 'Return to Sender', but by this time the contents was revealing itself as a very 'high' duck, too far gone for anyone's dinner, which had to be dumped. None of this damage would have occurred in the days of the old carriers.

The question of registration of parcels had not been worked out when the Rev. Charles L. Dodgson (alias Lewis Carroll) complained that he was unable to register valuable packets of drawings etc., which were too big for the letter-post. One hopes they were not any of the lovely 'Alice' ones that might have gone astray.

The problem of the delivery of parcels to their final destinations then came to a head. When the Royal Mail consisted of letters and perhaps newspapers it had been carried on foot, on horse-back, by Mail Cart and, for long distances, by coach, as we have seen. The carriage of parcels would require some other means of transport. 'Velocipedes' and tricycles were tried out and also a contraption known as 'the hen and chickens', which had a large wheel in the centre and smaller ones at each end, with big baskets attached. Resort was made to the use, once again, of coaches on some of the busy roads out of London. This was done under contract with a Post Office employee as guard, armed with a sword-bayonet and a revolver. These parcel mail coaches carried no passengers and travelled at night. The coachmen and guard were known as the 'pilgrims of the night'. They brought back nostalgic memories to the older people of the days of the mail coaches. The

A fine flock of 'Hens and Chickens' during the 1880s (The Post Office)

guard worked away all night, sorting the mails, blowing his post-horn to alert other night-time drivers of wagons of the Mail's approach and chatting with his own driver to keep him awake.

Royal Mail letter-carriers, now known for the first time, officially, as Postmen, were under great pressure, being expected to cope with the sudden influx of additional mail. It was not long before a poem appeared in *Punch* (29 September 1883) describing the plight of the rural carrier. I quote the first part:

An Old Postman's Story

Tis true, your honour, I'm fair dead beat, so I'll snatch a rest
  on this country stile.
For I've trudged and tramped with loaded back from county
  town 'tis many a mile
Up at the hour when the cock's awake and shuffling home
  when the bat's on wing,
A-calling here and a-calling there, with a wait for a knock
  and again for a ring:
A pleasant life do you call it, Sir? to skirt the hedges and
  brush the dew,
Well it's all very well for the folks in town, who come down
  here just to take their rest:
But with chaps like me when my labour's done and I long
  for leisure, then bed's the best.

It wasn't so bad in the days gone by, with letters tied up in a
    handy pack,
A stick, a satchel, a pair of legs, a sense of duty, a big, broad
    back:
But now it's different, quite, look here, when the grave is
    ready and sexton host
Let them bury me quiet, and put on the stone, 'His back it
    was broke by the Parcels Post'.

The authorities took this poem quite seriously, knowing that
Punch was read by influential people, many of them country dwell-
ers. But reaction soon set in. 'The rate of wage for rural
letter-carriers, say, 16s. a week all the year round for 16 single miles,
six days a week has not yet failed to get good men...We now...only
allow our men to carry 30 or 35 lbs....they say nothing about uniform, Xmas boxes and other advantages and little sources of income.'
And the hours worked—from about 5.45 a.m. to 9.30 a.m. and
from 3 p.m. to 7 p.m. gave postmen a nice long rest in between,
enabling them to 'find some occupation for which they receive pay
or food'. Was that official connivance at 'moonlighting'?

By the end of the century motorisation was on its way. In 1897
the Post Office was experimenting with motor vans driven by steam,
electricity and oil, with a variety of extraordinary vehicles. In 1899
a Daimler motor mail van took to the road, to great acclaim. During the 1914-18 war, when rubber for tyres was scarce, postmen on
pedal cycles often had to ride on the rims. Then, after the war,
with things beginning to get back to normal, the Post Office built
a fleet of thousands of vehicles. In the country motor cycles and
'combinations' were in use. Though horses were still on the move
in certain areas, such as the Highlands, by the 1950s the day of the
horse as the faithful carrier of the mails was over.

Today, we have a stock of the most splendid vehicles, from the
modest rural delivery vans to the enormous long-distance lorry, all
resplendent in shiny red paint, with golden crown and lettering
operating under the Parcel Force organisation of the Post Office.

There are certain rival operators, too, with alluring names and
symbols, the word 'Express' much used and arrows and pigeons,
perhaps standing for speed and direct delivery. The Post Office
does not have a monopoly of parcel delivery. In my experience the

125

standards of these alternative schemes do not match those of the official service. Their arrival time is not known, and parcels are left in odd places if one is out, with a note sometimes, not always, pushed into the keyhole or under the door. The drivers are mostly strangers to the area and frequently lose their way, get stuck down side-roads and have to be pulled out by tractor. Some refuse to tackle farm roads and leave goods 'to be collected' at the post office.

XXVII
The Post Takes to the Air

I shall always remember my astonishment one Sunday evening, in Skye, looking from the window and seeing people wandering past, Sunday newspapers tucked under their arms. Sunday newspapers on Sunday in Skye? It seemed incredible. Then, of course, I remembered. From Inverness by air Skye is the merest hop. This was long before the days of the bridge, when you travelled by train or car, waited for the ferry and had all the thrill of that crossing by sea which, short though it was, gave you the feel of going abroad, to a different country. I realised that though the Skye people could get Sunday papers on Sunday many would not read them till Monday. That was the custom.

Nowadays I have only to look up at the sky as I hear the sound of a plane, to think 'there goes my card. She'll get it in time for her birthday'. 'She' lives in London and her birthday begins in the morning, but I can be sure the greeting will be there in time. Acceleration of the mail must surely have reached an all-time high! Only once has this service to the south come to grief. One winter night of fog and rain, the plane crashed into a hillside quite soon after take-off. Luckily the pilot escaped death. The mail was scattered, but much of it was retrieved in daylight and returned, as far as practicable, to sender or sent on to the addressee, the Post Office always taking its duty seriously.

Have we really conquered the air? Man has been preoccupied with the idea of flight since the earliest times, his experiments often resulting in disaster. But he has persisted.

Long ago the Persians and the Arabs used homing pigeons for sending messages. This ensured an easy passage over enemy territory. It is said that swallows were used at one time in the East.

It is well known that pigeons played an important part in maintaining communications during the siege of Paris in 1870-71, when

An Imperial Airways mail-plane in 1935. An airmail van stands ready to transfer mail (The Post Office)

the Government had moved to Tours, in the south. The birds were transported, two or three at a time, in baskets attached to balloons. Official despatches were written by hand in minute letters, on tissue paper. The paper was rolled up and placed in a tiny tube which was tied either to the pigeon's leg or to one of its tail feathers. A waxed silk thread was used to minimise weight.

Micro-photography had been invented at this time. This allowed long messages to be sent in very small bulk. The pigeons had snow and frost to contend with. Many of them never reached their journey's end. Their services were highly valued during the long months of occupation.

Pigeons were used in peace-time, too, carrying messages between Auckland and the off-shore islands of New Zealand, until the extension of the telegraph service came along. The micro-filming of mail was used again during the Second World War by Britain and America, these letters being known as 'airgraphs.'

Another important factor in the development of aerial communication was the use of the balloon. During the siege of Paris, which lasted from mid-September 1870 until the end of January 1871 and was causing much misery and starvation, many balloons were able to leave the city in comparative safety, sailing over the heads of the Germans, anti-aircraft artillery not having been invented then. Some flights were nevertheless extremely hazardous and some ended fatally. Most of them carried mail, official and unofficial. Balloons had been invented at the end of the eighteenth century, hot-air balloons being superseded by those filled with inflammable gas. Ballooning became a craze in Europe and America. Some deliveries of mail were made by the early pioneers, but the unreliability of the balloon, which only needed a change of wind to go off course, precluded the setting-up of an official balloon mail service. During World War One the dirigible balloon, known as the 'Zeppelin', after its inventor, was used in bombing raids. Later, during the twenties and thirties Zeppelins did carry mail.

Meanwhile, much progress was being made in the development of flight by winged aircraft, both in Europe and America. The Post Office, always anxious to use new means of expediting the delivery of mail, was soon involved in the testing of these machines. The first flights were hazardous. Inevitably bad weather, engine trouble, forced landings in unknown territory—these were some of the hazards that had to be faced.

France had always been particularly keen to develop aviation. One famous pilot—Antoine de St Exupéry—flew the mails over the North African desert. He was so passionately devoted to flying that he could not live happily for any length of time on the ground. Several times he crashed in the desert and was rescued by Bedouin tribesmen. Even after suffering severe injuries he kept on flying. Eventually, he set off one day and did not return. No sign of him or his aircraft was ever found. He left us two marvellous books—*Terre des Hommes* and *Night Flight* in which he tries to tell something of what it meant to him to fly, his vision of the world below. He also wrote a story—*The Little Prince*—which can be read on the philosophical level of an adult or a child, as an allegory set among the stars.

The first airmail service in Britain was that between Inverness and Kirkwall, in Orkney. It was inaugurated on 29 May 1934, the plane piloted by Captain Eric Fresson, a great pioneer of aviation, whose statue now stands at the airport at Dalcross. After a frantic clearing of sheep off the runway at Kirkwall the plane landed safely, marking the start of a regular service.

Mails have been carried by glider, by radio-controlled pilot-less plane and have been dropped from the air by parachute, in canisters with a 'chute which opens only when it nears the ground, thus ensuring a soft landing. Helicopters are widely used to carry mail and, as we have seen, there have been experiments with rockets. In 1969 the Apollo XI crew took a letter to the moon and stamped and franked it there. What would St Exupéry have given to have been there!

There is no doubt that this conquest of the air and the development of aerial transportation have been greatly helped by aid and subsidies from postal administrations in many countries. Next stop the interplanetary mail!

XXVIII
Scarlet Coats and Ragged Trousers

Sometimes, on visits to the Head Office in town I would look wonderingly at the smart attire of the ladies at the counters—flowered blouses and well-cut skirts—the men in regulation shirt and trousers. Their bright appearance certainly did give one a feeling of confidence in their ability to ensure the safe expedition of one's mail to the trickiest corner of the planet, if not (yet!) to outer space. They were friendly, too, even though contact was minimal, just a smile from behind the grille and a glimpse of well-manicured fingers as they pushed your stamps and your change through the hollow below the bars. It must be a little like that when you visit someone in prison, I would think.

There was never a question of a uniform issue for the postmaster /mistress. Were we supposed to be a cut above the counter clerks and therefore able to dress as we liked, at our own expense? A flowered blouse and a well-cut skirt would seem a little out of place behind our old deal table, I thought, remembering the many times when I would hastily remove a kitchen or a garden apron as I hurried to answer a summons by the bell.

We were, however, issued with name badges in the late eighties, this at a time when personal identification had become imperative. They are certainly useful at meetings and conferences, but in my small sphere not strictly necessary for everyday use. I've been known to most of my customers for a good many years. Sometimes the badge is forgotten.

So—no uniform dress for me, but our postie sports his regulation navy outfit, with the scarlet piping at the pocket. For a while a light grey suit was tried out, but soon the navy blue was re-adopted.

131

I often envy him his wet-weather coat of yellow oilskin, guaranteed to keep out the wildest downpour.

Our young relief posties, once clear of the town, can adapt their uniform to suit themselves, or the weather. In summertime it's good to see them relaxed, shirt open at the neck, sleeves rolled high, clearly enjoying the round. One manages to pursue his hobby of photography, taking shots during his tea or lunch break. It's good to see these young men clearly finding pleasure in their day, with no fear of being assaulted or robbed, as their forerunners in the old times might have been. There was no question of an issue of clothing for the foot-posts. Many times they must have been soaked to the skin on the outward way with no time to dry off before the return. The mounted postboys did have headgear of a sort and big boots.

The earliest reference to postal clothing dates from 1590 when the Council of Aberdeen ordered for William Taylor, known as the 'Post', a livery of blue cloth, with the armorial bearings of the town worked in silver on his right sleeve. This was before the days of the state Postal Service and was purely a local organisation. Later, every letter-carrier was supposed to 'wear a brass ticket upon the most visible part of his clothing, with the king's arms upon the same'. I doubt whether this injunction was strictly obeyed everywhere.

When the mail coach service started in 1784, the Guards were provided with an official uniform—a scarlet coat with gold lapels and gold braid and a black hat with a gold band. The driver wore the same. Red was the royal colour and also the colour of the soldiers' uniforms. A military image was useful as a deterrent to the highwaymen who were always on the lookout for easy prey.

Letter-carriers in London were provided with uniforms in 1793. The men objected to this as it would mark them out as people carrying large sums of money and therefore make them liable to be attacked and robbed. However, they were over-ruled. One reason for the introduction of a uniform was the ragged condition of the letter-carriers' own clothes. So they were issued with a beaver hat, with gold band and cockade, scarlet coat (cut-away style) with blue lapels and cuffs, with brass buttons on which the wearer's number was inscribed and a blue cloth waistcoat. The uniform was to be renewed every year. They must have been a resplendent sight!

But...they were still required to provide their own trousers, so that 'It is recorded that the splendid coats and hats presented a strange contrast above the ragged cloaths of trousers which seem to have been not uncommon with the Letter Carriers of those days.' Some forty years later there was a suggestion that the letter-carriers should be supplied with waterproof capes as well to be attached to the coats as protection in bad weather, or that the coats should be made of waterproofed material. Both these ideas were turned down. Expense was probably the reason for the rejection of the ideas as there were by that time nearly 2,000 employees in several cities, including Edinburgh and Dublin, all issued with uniforms.

In 1855, at last, trousers were made part of the issue and waterproof capes, with scarlet frock coats, were provided. This must have been a welcome move. Not so welcome, however, was the adoption of the glazed tall hat as worn by the postmen of Paris. *Punch* got another word in on the subject, saying 'we hear that the new hat weighs very heavily on the heads of the Department on whose behalf we seriously suggest the removal of an invention which gives both heaviness and headache to a very meritorious class of public officers.' Sure enough, four years later it was superseded by a hard felt hat and then by a peaked cap.

The same issue of *Punch* had more to say regarding postmen's attire. Under the heading 'The Post Office in a Blaze' it said:

We lately had our eyes dazzled by the sight of the Postmen in a glaring red uniform, more fitted to the Fire Brigade than for a peaceful body of men connected with the department of *literae humaniores*, as the couriers of letters. We cannot comprehend the taste which has pinned a large pair of scarlet skirts to the coat of the Postman, and caused us to mistake him for a sentinel off his post, by his resemblance to a Foot Guardsman in one of the new regulation wrappers. Considering there is a Reward payable for the apprehension of a Deserter, we wonder that half the Postmen in London are not taken into custody every night on suspicion. We can see no necessity whatever for the military aspect of these men: and indeed in these war times it is enough to alarm half the old women of London to have their portals thundered at every hour of the day by men of military aspect. We recommend the immediate abolition of this very martial attire, by elevating the Postman into a very formidable rival to the Policeman, in those little flirtations with our female servants, which have often kept a sentimental Constable grunting hoarse nothings into our housemaid's ear, while some burglarious gentleman has been emptying our neighbour's plate-chest. The Post Office is in every respect a Model Department, and the new costume has probably not originated from its heads, which are too much occupied with improving our means of communication to be able to bestow much time on the cut and colour of the Postman's attire.

Punch also fabricated a petition from the wives of Postmen regarding the non-issue of trousers to their husbands. Thus:

To her Gracious Majesty the Queen: the humble petition of the Wives of the Postmen—Madam, May it please your gracious goodness to look with a smiling eye upon the husbands of your Petitioners. Your gracious goodness supplies to 'em from the Crown a coat, a waistcoat, a hat with a band which only the illiterate multitude take for gold. Your Petitioners pray that the Crown would not leave off at the waistcoat, but continue its bounty in the way of trousers and end it with shoes...Your Petitioners humbly appeal to your Majesty's sympathies as a wife. What would be your Majesty's feelings to see Prince Albert in the fine laced coat of a General, with shabby trousers and boots not fit for any painter to take him in?

One wonders if copies of *Punch* ever reached the tea-table at the Palace or Balmoral? Gradually the issue of uniforms was extended to the Provinces, the Surveyor of Manchester pointing out that 'it is important to the safety of correspondence posted in the pillar boxes (these were proliferating) that anyone seen opening a pillar should at once be recognised by the public as our servant'. Thereafter all Post Office employees were provided with uniforms.

Soon the London letter-carriers were getting two pairs of trousers and a new hat each year, also two coats a year, and waistcoats and capes every two years. The provinces did less well. There was still no mention of trousers, only one hat and two coats a year and a cape biennially. Then, in 1861,

as it had been found that the scarlet uniforms of the Letter Carriers very quickly became soiled, this colour was discarded, in
favour of: A blue coat with scarlet collar and cuffs and scarlet
piping—the letters G.P.O. above the wearer's number being
embroidered in white on each side of the collar. A blue vest
similarly piped with scarlet. Blue winter trousers, with a broad
scarlet stripe. The summer trousers, in grey, with a scarlet cord
stripe.

A few years later the frock-coat was replaced by a tunic of military
pattern. In Edinburgh and London a tunic with tails was adopted,
as the letter-carriers were required to do so much stair-climbing
that it was often inconvenient for them to wear their greatcoats
and the tail-coat gave them the necessary protection from the cold.

In 1870 the Telegraph companies were taken over by the Post
Office and the boy messengers were supplied with uniforms. Soon
the rural letter-carriers were equipped with standard dress. During
the 1914-18 war many women joined the Post Office Department.
They were issued with a blue cap and blue straw hat, blue serge
skirt and cape and boots.

Some day, I promise myself, I will take a trip to the Post Office
Museum in London to see some of these marvellous uniforms of
the past. Looking at our postie of today, well-equipped in his neat,
blue outfit, with boots and a waterproof coat as protection against
any kind of weather, I think of the days of the ragged trousers
topped by the scarlet frock-coats with the top hats and wonder
how his predecessors ever managed their rounds in such theatrical
garb.

XXIX
More Highland Post Offices

One summer, staying for a few nights in a Bed and Breakfast establishment, in one of the islands, I met a couple who were 'collecting' small Highland Post Offices. This meant photographing them and showing them to friends as mementoes of their holiday. The town-dweller of today is accustomed to find the local post office a place one goes to for the carrying-out of somewhat boring, business-like transactions. Coming across a small tin shack on the edge of the beach in one of the islands with the familiar label, in the familiar design, 'Post Office' stuck above the door, or perhaps the Gaelic 'Offis a'Phuist', he is amazed.

We have had encounters of this kind ourselves. Pushing open the door, we look round. There is a counter, some rather tattered posters and notices on the walls, no sign of an official. A child comes in.

'Sorry. Gran will be here in a minute' she says, with a shy smile.

A moment or two later an elderly woman appears, wiping her hands on her apron. 'You've not been waiting long, I hope. Morag said she saw you coming across the sands. I was just chasing a cow from the garden.'

'No. That's all right. We've only just arrived.'

'And are you on holiday?'

'Yes. We're staying a few days.'

'You like it here?' She gives us a quizzical look. 'It can be fearful wild sometimes.'

'We like it. Tell me...What's the name of the castle over there, at the head of the bay?'

She smiles, almost apologetically. 'Ach, that's just a ruin. The MacLeods had it long ago. It's called Castle Leod, for them. Are you quite comfortable where you are staying?' The present day is clearly of more importance to her than the past, with its memories of betrayal.

'Yes, we're very happy.'

'That's good, then.' By now she is composed, smiling and at her place behind the counter. Morag was regarding us with half-concealed curiosity.

'Has Morag far to go to school?' We could see no sign of a building looking like a school, only a few scattered houses, no shop, no church.

'About twelve miles. There's a mini-bus to take the children. But she has had the toothache and her not sleeping.'

'Oh, dear. That's sore.' Morag gives a half smile. Here we were, in the middle of someone's day, with a cow in the garden and a child's sore tooth. The transacting of business seemed relatively unimportant. But we did need stamps.

'Och, yes. Now wait a minute. I've some nice new ones. They came the other day.'

She hunts in a drawer and we exclaim with delight at the beauty of the fresh issue. 'You like them? I have others.' She turns the pages of the old stamp-book. It is a replica of our own. Feeling guilty at not disclosing the fact that we, too, run a post office, but not wishing to embarrass her, we pick out several attractive pictorials.

'We don't sell so many of them. Folk here seem to like the plain ones better.'

'Are you kept fairly busy?'

'Not what you'd really call busy, I suppose. Not like I've seen them in Fort William when I was there one day. But the pensioners need an office here. They could never travel twelve miles to collect their pensions. And they often get big parcels. They buy from the catalogues. And there's the phone here. And they like a wee blether.'

'Of course. Are there many?'

'Quite a few. They like to stay on in their old homes, even though the young couples move in to keep the ground worked. They like their independence. And...they love the place.'

'I can understand that.' We gather up our stamps and settle the bill, amazed at how quickly the postmistress adds up the amount. 'That was fast work!'

She smiles. 'We did lots of arithmetic in our heads. I've never forgotten.'

'Were you at school here?'

An islander collecting his pension in the Isle of Coll post office
(The Post Office)

'I was. It was just a wee school. Called a side school. It took a kind of overflow from the bigger one where Morag goes now. In fact...it was in this very building.'

'Goodness!'

'It was. There was just about a dozen of us. We had desks and slates and some books. Sometimes the rain came in the roof, but we had a wonderful teacher.'

'Well, that's...'

'Excuse me now. I see the post coming. He'll be ready for his tea. He has the nurse with him. She'll be going to see Mrs Mackinnon and she'll get a lift back with him when he's finished.' Sure enough, on the nearby road the small red van has drawn up and the post is making his way down, a large bundle of packages on his back. The catalogue buys, we reckon.

'Thanks then. And goodbye. All the best.'

'Goodbye. Haste ye back!' Morag smiles again, confidently now.

We leave reluctantly, greeting the postie as we pass. Gazing round at the sea, with the small waves breaking on the dazzling sand, at the distant curve of hills and breathing in the scent of the machair and its flowers, we're glad there are those clinging to the place they love and making room for the young to follow. We remember, as they do, all those others who had to leave. We're thankful there's a place, a small focal point, where their needs are understood and can be seen to cheerfully, a tiny post office, in a tin hut by the beach.

If you want to get the feel of a place this is where to come, to the small post office, the smaller the better. It is nearly always run by somebody local who has lived there all his, or her, life. The hotel, if there is one, is most often run by an incomer or an employee of a big group. He'll give you the statistics—the height of the hill, the state of the tides, where to get your fishing permit and so on, but he'll speak with the accent of Glasgow or Leeds and his bright young assistants will be from Australia or New Zealand and will be gone by the end of summer.

These small post offices were only set up with a struggle. In the early nineteenth century, when contact with the south and its commercial enterprises was increasing rapidly the need for postal services was also increasing. The lairds, as we have seen, were active in promoting the development of these services, since it was greatly to their benefit to do so. Postal services were to mean more than the provision of a runner, or letter-carrier from the nearest town.

One of the earliest offices to be established in the north was at Balbair, in Easter Ross, in October 1843. It was a Receiving Office, and Andrew Ross, the Receiver, along with the villagers, guaranteed to meet any expenses incurred by the Post Office. The office remained in the same building for many years. A Mrs Ross, sub-postmistress in 1966, reckoned that the premises she worked in were the very ones in which the original office had been set up. This Balbair sub-office was renamed Edderton in 1879 and in that same year, during the night of the Tay Bridge disaster, its original thatched roof was blown off. The Post Office was subsequently moved into the village shop and later it was taken into the hotel where it is worked on a part-time basis.

At Crathie, near Balmoral in Aberdeenshire, a Receiving Office was established in September 1842, a Mr Anderson as guarantor of the Post Office expenses of £5 a year. The first Receiver was Charles Thomson, head forester on the Balmoral estate. Realising that the introduction of the Universal Penny Post of 1840 would mean a large increase in the volume of mail, he had set about building a post office, combined with a house. It was of the usual traditional style of cottage and barely furnished, a wooden dresser having a special drawer for the post office equipment. Charles Thomson carried on the business here for 45 years, until his death in 1887. Queen Victoria, who was an inveterate letter-writer, visited the post office regularly. She refrained from using the royal prerogative of franking, that is, non-payment of postage, though some of her letters were sent by royal couriers. After Charles Thomson died she wanted his son Albert to take over the office, but Albert was following a successful career in London. The queen, not to be outdone, undertook personally to make up any deficiency in income which the change of job might bring and he was duly installed as postmaster by royal request! Later, she saw to it that two rooms were added to the building and the post office moved to the new wing.

After 43 years service Albert died and his widow took over the office until her eldest son, another Albert—a favourite name at the time!—was appointed postmaster in 1947. He and his brother Gordon carried on the business for many years in the same building which had been the family home for over a century. The thousands of tourists who flock to Crathie every summer have certainly made good use of the postal facilities there. It is often the case, as recorded in the Post Office Archives, that a rural office remains in the hands of the same family for several generations and often in the same building.

In our own area there are several houses which are known, or were known—two have been demolished—as the 'old' post office. I can count four before it came to the schoolhouse, where it has been for close on fifty years, with postmasters of the same family for close on forty. Records show that Abriachan had a date stamp in 1904, so it has been in the annals for nearly one hundred years.

As regards the 'Head' post office for the area, the office in Inverness, it had a chequered history, too. A Miss Helen McCulloch is in the records as having the title Postmistress in Inverness in 1737 and was said to be responsible for all letters despatched north of the Firth of Forth. Mr Penrose Hay, postmaster, who published in 1885 a short book called *Post Office Recollections*, says:

> in and prior to 1790 the head Post Office of the town was situated at what is now 32 Castle Street, when the whole business was easily disposed of in a room 14 feet by 9 feet 6 ins. The

Inverness Post Office, by Pierre Delavault (courtesy of *Inverness Courier*)

aperture for the letter-box was in the old window shutter and, as there was no coach beyond Inverness, neither was there any bridge, the mails to and from Dingwall, Caithness and Skye were conveyed on a pony ridden by old William Smith, afterwards Bellman and Shoremaster. The ponies used for the purpose were stabled in rear of his premises in Castle Street.

The townspeople would call at the Receiving Office to collect their letters. On market day the names of people from the country for whom a letter had arrived would be called out.

About 1810 the post office was moved to a more central place, near the 'Exchange'. Ten years later it was moved again, to a house in Church Street, on the corner with Bank Lane. The office covered about 110 square feet. The letter-box measured exactly 4 inches by ¼-inch. Letters of that time were of a single sheet so the aperture was adequate. We are fortunate in having a sketch of this old post office and of the letter-box, done by Pierre Delavault, who was art master at the Academy and made sketches of many of the old buildings of Inverness, most of which have now, sadly, been demolished.

The staff in this old post office consisted of the postmaster and one letter-carrier. Business was not brisk. Mr Hay says: 'I recollect distinctly of the postmaster going away in that year (1829) for a twelve hours holiday, leaving the whole department in charge of the one old letter carrier, who discharged the whole duties of the day most satisfactorily'. This is certainly extraordinary as the letter-carriers were Gaelic speakers and mostly more or less illiterate. How the letters reached their destinations has always been a mystery.

In 1841, the year after the Universal Penny Post came in, the post office was transferred to Baron Taylor's Lane. There were then four postmen. A few years later it went to a substantial building in the High Street, where a Victorian letter-box in the wall is still in use. Post office business was increasing rapidly and the staff soon rose to sixty-three. By 1890 premises in Queensgate had been specially built to accomodate the post office, with a staff of one hundred. The present building, modernised and equipped to a high standard, is on the site of this Victorian model. This is the place whose portals we enter from time to time, to marvel at its weighing and stamping devices, at its safety measures, at its orderly queue, at its tidily uniformed staff. We return to our own small corner with a slight sigh of relief.

Next morning I give the floor an extra careful sweep, polish the brasses till they gleam, tidy the piles of leaflets, put some flowers on the window ledge. Standards must be seen to.

XXX
Post Office Cats

An essential member of any country household is a cat. Two is an even more desirable number and can usually be quite quickly achieved. Country mice, which usually take up their abode in warm corners of the house by late autumn, can do an amazing amount of damage. One winter we had a plague of rats, when a neighbour found water coming through his kitchen ceiling, the hungry rodents having chewed through the plastic piping in the loft. Mice can attack electric wiring, too. That particular year we had to call in the Pest Officer.

Normally our cat, who is a great hunter, often catching young hares bigger than herself, is sufficient deterrent. Sometimes, alas, she kills birds and once or twice, with a puzzled expression in her eyes, she has dumped a small lizard at my feet. Her main job is to keep the mice in subjection and that she does work hard to achieve. They love paper, these small rodents, and can eat their way through plastic containers, too. With the multiplicity of forms coming into the office, cramming the drawers where they are lodged, I have to think of ways to protect them from possible onslaught. Tin boxes are the only mouse-proof containers and they are hard to come by.

In older times post office equipment was more vulnerable to attack than its modern type. Mail-bags were of canvas and made quite a tasty bite for a hungry rat. Even leather travelling cases were not immune. Leave the catch half open and the mice would be in, nesting cosily among the letters. The authorities were quick to see that measures must be taken to protect valuable documents of all kinds from attack by destructive rodents.

The Post Office Archives have a most evocative account of the introduction of cats onto the premises as a means of controlling vermin. By courtesy of these Archives I am tempted to quote at some length from their Information Sheet called 'Cats on the Payroll.'

In September 1868 the Controller of the Money Order Office in London asked the Secretary of the Post Office for authority to pay two shillings per week for the maintenance of three cats. The Secretary's reply reads: 'Three cats may be allowed on probation—they must undergo a test examination and should, I think, be females. It is important that the cats be not overfed and I cannot allow more than one shilling per week for their support—they must depend on the mice for the remainder of their emoluments and if the mice be not reduced in number in six months a further portion of the allowance must be stopped.

A further minute to the Secretary, later in the month, reads:

These directions have been communicated to Tye [the Resident Porter] who will no doubt find means to inform the cats upon what terms they are to be employed and what is expected of them...it is hoped that the cat movement will be successful.

On 5 May 1869 the Secretary, having called for a report on the cats, was told

whether influenced by the Secretary's caution that they would under certain contingencies have diminished rations or by a laudable zeal for the service and their own character, cannot clearly be made out, but it is certain that the Cat System has answered exceedingly well, and that the cats have done their duty very efficiently, except as respects one point of the Secretary's order which implied a probable increase to that portion of the Establishment.'

The following suggestion was put to the Secretary:

...in the event of a Committee of Inspection being appointed I would suggest that Tye's evidence should be taken as to the test examination. I understand he can explain the reason why the cats have not acted up to orders in the matter of increasing the Establishment.

In 1873 the postmaster at Southampton was refused an allowance of one shilling and ninepence per week for a cat. He protested, saying:

> Mr. Wadman, the Guard...argues that such a sum would be quite insufficient. He says no nourishment can be derived from rats which reside in the Post Office store-room: that picking such rats, fed as they are upon nothing but Mail Bags, is no better than picking Oakum...

He (Mr Wadman) also complains about 'the loss of dignity in carrying the cats' food through the streets in her Majesty's uniform' and demands compensation for this. But no increase was granted.

In 1877 several cat allowances were granted, in Nottingham, Deptford and in the Post Office Headquarters in London. In February 1919 a Report from the Accountant General's Department, Telephone House, London reads:

> a few telegrams have been eaten away by mice to such an extent as to be useless. Beyond the inconvenience caused by the mutilation of forms, etc. I have no particular objections but some of the ladies are rather perturbed. How about instituting an office cat?

Later, he appealed: 'at least two cats seem to be necessary...'

Questions in the House 1953

On 18th. March 1953 the Assistant Postmaster General was asked, during question time in the House of Commons, 'when the allowance payable for the maintenance of cats in his Department was last raised, what is the total amount involved: what is the present rate per cat in Northern Ireland: and how this compares with the rate in London?' He replied: 'There is, I am afraid, a certain amount of industrial chaos in the Post Office cat world. Allowances vary in different places, possibly according to the alleged efficiency of the animal and other factors. It has proved impossible to organise any scheme for payment by results or output bonus. These servants of the state are, moreover, frequently unreliable, capricious in their duties and liable to prolonged absenteeism...There are no post office cats in Northern Ireland. Except for cats at Post Office Head-quarters who got the special allowance a few years ago, presumably for prestige reasons, there has been a general wage freeze since July 1918, but there have been no complaints!' The member then asked: 'How does my honourable friend account for the fact that no allowances are payable for cats in Northern Ireland? Is it because the post offices there are more sanitary, and will he say what happens if a cat has kittens? Is there a family allowance payment?' The Assistant Post Master General replied: 'There are no cats in Northern Ireland, I presume, be-cause there are no mice in post office buildings. With regard to the children's allowances I'm afraid there is none. But the Head Postmasters have full discretion to give a maternity grant...' He was then asked by a lady member whether 'this is one of the occasions on which equal pay prevails?' to which he replied 'Equal pay has been accepted both in principle and in practice.'

Celebrity Cats

In December 1964, to the distress of the staff, Tibs, the giant official cat of the Post Office Headquarters Building, who weighed 23 lbs., died, after 14 years' service. His wages had been 2/6d. a week and his office was in the old St. Martin's Refresh-ment Club in the basement. He had his photograph in the book 'Cockney Cats'.

Famous among Post Office cats of 1968 were Persil, who protected Dial House in Manchester, and Chippy, who looked after the Supplies Department in Bridgwater. Persil sometimes took only two hours to patrol his huge building, but when, in 1968, he had attained 13 years of age, he did take the lift be-tween floors. Chippy's only fault was that he frequently got into one of the railway vans bound for the neighbouring town of Taunton, when his keeper had to go and bring him back.

In April 1971 a strange, obviously lady cat, was observed wandering along the basement corridors and rooms of Post Office Headquarters building, trying to find a suitable place to call 'home'. She was provided with food and milk and very soon produced a litter of five sturdy kittens. One of the male kittens, black and white in colour, was kept for duty at Headquarters. The new post office employee was given the name Blackie and taught to catch mice by his adept mother. Over the years that followed Blackie did a magnificent job in keeping Headquarters mouse-free...In June 1983 the Personnel Manager for Post Office Headquarters, John Roxby, pleaded to the Post Office Pay Group for an increase in Blackie's pay, the Cats' Official Allowance having stood at £1 a week, unreviewed, since 1967. Top level pay talks were quickly held and a pay award of 100% awarded to Blackie and all post office cats.

These extracts show, I think, that the postal authorities were basically humane and certainly had a good sense of humour! The story of Post Office cats, an illustrated history, has been told in a book by Russell Ash—*Dear Cats: The Post Office Letters*.

XXXI
The Red Letter-box

Looking from the door at the bright red letter-box firmly attached to a solid wooden post at the roadside, I often think what a useful purpose it serves. Every morning postie opens it and deposits the contents on the counter. 'Not much today' he'll say, or 'someone's been busy!' as a whole lot with addresses in the same hand appears. I tie the letters into a bundle and put them into his safe grip. Sometimes I wonder what he's carrying off on the first stage of their journey to...Aberdeen, London, Canada, Australia—what news, accounts of events, messages of hope, perhaps of despair. That small letter-box has carried them all in its day. It sits there, so accessible, subject to the ravages of the west wind, the rain, snow and frost. From time to time it gets a much-needed coat of fresh paint.

I remember the letter-boxes in the islands where the birds are allowed to make their home at nesting-time and where benighted travellers stop to read the name of the location and to find they are at least on the map. That happens with our letter-box, too. Young walkers, in the summer, tired from their trek up the hill road, slip off their gigantic packs, peer at the name on the box and slump down for a rest among the flowers on the bank. 'A b r i a c h a n' they chant, putting the wrong accent on the wrong syllable and defeated by the sound of 'ch'.

'That must be somewhere.'

'Maybe it's on the map.'

'We'll see later. I'm for a drink.'

'There's not much water left.'

'There's a house in there, behind the hedge.'

'A house?'

'M'm...'

Next moment I'm filling water-bottles and pointing out camping-

A Victorian rectangular letter-box

places and receiving thanks with friendly smiles. The letter-box has done its little trick again!

In older times letters were often left at inns or other meeting places known to be frequented by the recipient, a sort of unofficial *poste restante* system. I have seen a letter written soon after the battle of Culloden and addressed to its recipient at the Laigh Coffee House, Edinburgh.

After the introduction of the Penny Post there was, of course, a tremendous number of letters written. People had already been asked to provide slots in their front doors to speed the delivery of incoming mail. Now, Post Office officials set about installing boxes for the outward despatch of letters in the streets of the towns and at places on the roadside in the country. France provided the example for this facility. In 1851 Anthony Trollope, then a mere Surveyor's clerk, proposed that the scheme operating in France should be tried out in Jersey. It was. Next year the postmaster in St Helier reported that 'the Roadside letter-boxes work satisfactorily', and in England 'they must be introduced liberally and energetically...' In St Peter Port, Guernsey, a hexagonal pillar box 4 feet 8 inches high, erected in 1853, is still in use today.

The first one to appear on the mainland, in that same year, was at Carlisle. Two years later the first boxes were installed in London. They were sturdy, rectangular boxes, about 5 feet in height. After public complaints about the ugly appearance of these boxes an official invitation to submit an improved design was issued to the Department of Science and Art. The result was some very ornate specimens, with intertwined leaves and the Royal Cipher prominently displayed.

Pillar boxes in the county towns, which were emptied less frequently than those in London, were soon found to be inadequate for the ever-increasing amount of mail. A larger size had to be introduced. All these boxes were dark green in colour. In 1874 red was adopted. This made the boxes easily distinguishable. Over the next ten years boxes everywhere were painted red. In France yellow is the preferred colour, in Ireland bright green. Red, as noted earlier, has always been the royal colour in Britain.

As there were many complaints of letters being caught up in the internal structure of the hexagonal boxes and so delayed, the cylindrical, or pillar, shape was re-introduced. Still there were complaints that larger letters and newspapers became lodged in the tops of these new boxes, as garments become lodged in washing-machines today. The posting aperture was thereafter placed a few inches lower in the body of the box. Strangely, it was not until eight years after their introduction that it was realised the boxes did not bear the Royal Cipher nor any indication that they were Post Office property. Thereafter the letters V.R. and the words 'Post Office' were incorporated in the design.

In 1912 the Postmaster General observed that pillar boxes were 'unsightly objects and that in these days of Town Planning and Municipal Aesthetics we ought to show better examples of art applied to postal uses.' Students of the Royal College of Art were invited to submit designs, but the First World War broke out and adoption of any of the designs chosen had to be suspended.

Today our town pillar boxes look very similar to those of close on a hundred years ago, with the addition of a plaque showing the times of collection and, in some cases, a machine for buying stamps. In Inverness there are several letter boxes of a different type—set into solid stone walls and bearing the Royal Cipher—V.R. for Victoria. Aberdeen has two Edward VIII pillar boxes. In the Inverness Museum are two old letter-boxes. One, called a Lamp letter-box,

The Author with the letter-box at Abriachan (John H. Paul Photography)

has a socket for a lamp attached to the side of the depository for letters. There are other old Post Office artefacts in the Museum—a post horn used on the mail coach, old scales, a hand cart. The interest in all aspects of the history of postal services is such that study groups have been set up covering various facets. One of these is the Letter Box Study Group which keeps updated information and listing of interesting boxes of which there must be many up and down the country. Letter-boxes, like other street furniture—seats, litter bins and so on—are prominent features of a townscape. It's important that their design strikes easy on the eye.

XXXII
Computers Don't Bite

As the advent of the millenium drew nearer and nearer, with the brilliance of technology growing brighter and brighter, I began to think seriously about my place in the great scheme of things. I fingered my identity badge. Did this small piece of plastic add anything to my stature? Not really. Most often I forgot to put it on. Postal instructions continued to pour in, their plastic folders cluttering every available shelf and drawer. I perused them before filing them away, but they really contained little relevance to the situations encountered here. The insuring of certain packages to a country in the Middle East was something seldom, if ever, asked for in this particular office.

A video was circulated among the small offices. The sight and sound of all those highly efficient people working away among the forms and documents with which they appeared so alarmingly at ease, only added to one's feeling of inadequacy. Then I remembered—probably these people never had to deal with lost travellers, with road accidents or sudden death, or even with sad folk in need of a listening ear. A reading of the Postmaster's Contract made one realise how fastidiously correct the rules of employment had to be. The rate of compensation for the loss of half a finger, compared to that for the loss of a thumb, in the course of one's work, how could it be calculated? Attendance at meetings of other rural postmasters/mistresses was useful. We could discuss somewhat similar problems, though none of them were quite as rural as us. Most of them had a small shop attached and were familiar with the workings of V.A.T., advertising, consumer protection and other quantities unknown to me. Some friendly conversation over a meal was cheering. Then I got back to my corner, to be greeted by my cat and to change the date-stamp in readiness for the morning.

The arrival of Willy-the-Post was always a bright occasion. His never-failing cheerfulness put a smile on the day, as it did for every

Passengers on board the Post Bus (The Post Office)

house he visited on his round. Sometimes he would have a younger man with him, a trainee learning the routine work for future employment as a holiday relief. It's good to know that some younger people are coming into the business. A country round in the Highlands must surely be an attractive proposition. It means early rising, as many jobs do. Once you're away in your little red van, out of the town and up the hill road into the sweet air, the day is yours. You can be sure of a welcome in every house you call at, a laugh and a crack, a hot drink in winter, a cool one in summer, a tractor to pull you out of a snowdrift or a pool of mud. Then you're finished for a long evening of freedom. You may not make a monetary fortune, but who can count the price of glimpsing a pine marten as he flashes into the wood, a fox standing bright-eyed by the road, roe-deer in Tom Fraser's turnips, these are the early morning sightings to be enjoyed at no other time. Later, the buzzards will be on the move, gliding serenely above their prey, and, if it's a lucky day, there may be whoopers on the loch, or heron, or a little grebe.

There are the personal encounters, too, apart from those on the doorstep. The lone bird-watcher whose bike has sprung a puncture may flag the post bus for a lift. A foreign tourist, always forgetting which side to drive on, may well collide with a truck emerging from a croft road. The post bus comes in handy for a pull to clear the way and perhaps the loan of tools from its well-stocked bag. It's all part of the service!

One day our trainee met a couple from Poland who stopped him to ask the way. Their English was halting. He made his explanations as clearly as he could and was for moving on. They wouldn't let him go. They walked round the van, their eyes shining with admiration. The woman pointed to the lettering and ran her fingers round the golden crown. 'Please, what it means, "Royal Mail"? You have letters from the Queen?' That made a good story for his mates!

The days passed happily into summer that year. The children came to borrow books from the library. The holidays brought the usual influx of visitors from far and wide. Avid stamp collectors would stand goggle-eyed as I turned the pages of the stamp book for them.

'You have some of those? What luck! I just need two to complete another set.'

The Scottish standard issue, with the special little lion rampant, was much sought after. And the pound notes were prized.

'We don't see many of them now,' a southerner would say. I began to feel Scotland was 'abroad' to them! People came, as always, looking for their roots. Standing at the gate, they would gaze around at the small tumbled ruins, at the re-built houses, at the modern designs, at the barren fields.

'I guess folks today think maybe more about their houses than about the ground they live on,' one Canadian visitor said, with sadness in his voice. 'I've heard the stories my grandad told, of how it was a handful of earth they took with them across the Atlantic. That was the most precious thing to them, their land. They could build a house most anywhere. That's what they had to do on arrival, build a house, not out of stone, but out of the trees they had to cut down.'

'Yes. I know what you mean.'

We're gazing now, both of us, at the little fields over the road, with the tumble-down fences, rushes and heather encroaching, where oats and potatoes, roots and pasture would have kept life going along quite happily a century ago. I remembered how one elderly visitor from Ireland, gazing at it a few years ago, had said,

with infinite sadness in his voice, 'Oh the lovely valley that's in it!'
That's what it was—a 'hanging valley', left behind when the ice slid
down into the big hollow below. Alas, now, it was uneconomic to
put money into small agricultural units that would each only serve
the needs of one family.

I came out of my day-dream. The Canadian was still lost in his.
Then—'Tell me about those clearances' he said. I told him what I
knew. It would be a long time in the telling, the whole story.

'But this is not a place that was cleared. This is a place people
came to after they were cleared from the fertile glens.'

'So they had to start all over again, from scratch?'

'They did. They carved those fields out of the heather. They
worked hard to provide for the next generation.'

'And then the young ones left?'

'They did well. There was always a good school here. And they
took jobs in the town or emigrated voluntarily.'

'So now you have a new kind of Highlander.'

'You could say that. We're lucky here. Only two or three of
the old families remain, but the newcomers are understanding. They
look to the future for their children's sake but they don't ignore
the past.'

He is still deep in thought, then he turns to shake my hand.

'My, am I glad you had time to talk to me about all this. I'll be
telling them back home. Goodbye now and God speed.' The post
office bell rings. Someone had come in by the side gate.

'Goodbye to you. God bless.' I hurry back to the office. A
family allowance is due. And there are parcels. A car comes into
the yard, reverses, turns, parks. It is not one I recognise. A small
lady emerges and stands quietly by the door, as though forming the
start of a queue. I finish stamping the parcels and see my customer
off. The lady comes in. I know her now. My 'guardian angel' I call
her, the person I can call on in any emergency, who can be 'paged'
and contacted wherever she may be.

'You're busy' she says, with a warm smile.

So she hasn't come with news of office closures, not with a
smile like that. Has she? Or could she be going to discuss the possi-
bility of our becoming a Community Office? I didn't want that. I
knew my customers would never remember which days and at
what times the office was open. Community offices are open only

on certain days and at certain times. What about the retired academic who lived at the top of the hill and came every day to collect his mail, on skis in the winter? There was a road of sorts to his place, but he came down every day. He liked it that way. And our geologist who used to tell people it took him a couple of hours to buy a stamp. How's that, they would say, there must be a long queue! No, no, but by the time I've had a cup of coffee and read the papers the time's up! he'd grin. So—no community office here.

'I was just passing' my lady says 'so I came in to see if there was anything you were needing.'

'Thanks. No, I think everything's all right.'

'You will have heard about the computerisation?'

Computerisation? Dreaded word.

'Er...no, not really.'

'Every office is to be on the system. Soon.'

'Oh? Even this one? How soon?'

She smiles again. 'Quite soon, I think. It's not exactly certain yet. They're marvellous machines. Make everything so quick and simple.'

'Quick and simple'. That's it, I thought. That's what machines do. But do we really want everything to be quick and simple? What about the hours, days, months, years those monks on Iona spent on their daily job of producing illuminated manuscripts which are now priceless treasures? One day the machines will produce works of art? And we shall sit back and watch? I come back to the conversation in hand.

'I'm not very handy with machines' I apologise.

'Don't worry. There's nothing to it. You'll see. Goodbye, now. I'm off to the islands today.'

'To the islands? Which ones?'

'To the small ones. Raasay first.' Raasay my well-loved island!

'And they will be computerised?'

'Eventually, yes. Remember the slogan—"computers don't bite"!'

'I'm sure they don't. But I believe they can make mistakes!'

'That's not really their fault. You'll see. Don't worry. See you soon.'

With a wave and a smile she slips into her car and is off. So the millennium and its technology is on the way. But there has been no mention of office closures. Perhaps we can survive!

XXXIII
Links with the Future

The imminent arrival of computerisation to the office made me realise that I must forge links with the future. The present had always seemed good enough for me, especially on a warm, blue day in summer, even on an ice-cold one in winter, on every kind of day really. The past held a special kind of fascination for me, as I saw it here, before my eyes, and held it in my hand in the shape of our venerable date-stamp or an old iron griddle on its way to the museum collection.

The future I was leaving in the capable hands of my grandchildren. They were all, even the youngest, computer experts, I knew. E-mail, fax machines, the web, the internet, held no mystery or terror for them. They were fluent in the new language of technology, too. Language is another of my loves, but this one holds little attraction. Nevertheless, I began to feel it was incumbent on me to learn the rudiments. Did it have a grammar? Not really, I reckoned, just a plethora of strange words—nouns and verbs made out of them. Thus—to computerise.

At least I could gather some statistics to find out which way the Post Office was going. I had seen signs of competing structures— fleets of vans named 'Northern Express', 'Highland Delivery', 'Pegasus Express', even one calling itself a 'Courier'. I knew the Post Office held no monopoly for parcel delivery. These vehicles were quite impressive but not as smart as our own Parcel Force vans.

The Post Office Archives in London have provided me with much very valuable information about all aspects of the history of the postal service. For the picture of modern times in Scotland I turned to the Scottish Post Office Board in Edinburgh. The Board covers the four branches—Royal Mail, Post Office Counters, Parcel Force and Subscription Services (telemarketing). In a foreword to its information brochure it states: 'The Post Office...has a long tradition of strong social commitment, particularly to rural areas.' That statement cheered me at once. Then I read that 'over 92% of first class letters posted for delivery in Scotland are delivered next day. There are over 2,000 post offices in the country, with 3.5 million customers a week. Parcel Force handles 140 million parcels a year, its world-wide network covering 239 countries. In 1995-96 Royal Mail handled 17.5 billion items of mail'. The mind shivers!

The technology used in processing the mail is now of the highest order. Looking ahead the report says: 'In the not-too-distant future delivery postmen will be able to come to work and find their mail already sorted, house by house, into correct walk sequence.'

The Post Office Act of 1969 changed the status of the Post Office from that of a Government Department to that of a Public Corporation, and a Post Office Users' National Council was set up as an independent watch-dog. There are Post Office Advisory Councils so that customers' complaints and advice can be heeded. Consultation with these bodies always precedes changes in prices or service. Consumer protection is clearly a priority in the management of the Post Office, the Royal Mail Customer Service always at hand.

What cheered me most in the Board's report was the account of the efforts made to oversee environmental issues. Investment projects are required to include a detailed environmental impact statement. There are trials on ways of reducing the impact of road vehicles by using fuel oil made from rape seed, low sulphur diesel, electric-powered vans and the VW Ecomatic vehicle, designed to minimise noise and exhaust gases. Parcel Force has fitted excessive-speed limiters on its large trucks to save fuel.

In 1995 a collection and recycling scheme for Christmas cards run by the Post Office resulted in the equivalent of over 5,000 trees being planted. The reduction in landfill costs meant that savings were used to plant 2,760 trees in community forests throughout the United Kingdom.

Post Office Counters conducted environmental surveys with suppliers to identify their level of commitment to care of the environment. They also continued to identify ways of reducing waste and minimising harmful environmental effects in the production of its stationery and leaflets. I was particularly glad to read this as I had always thought small offices such as ours would benefit from a reduction in the number of leaflets received. The rain-forests of the world would benefit, too.

Parcel Force has developed a new type of label to replace the current four-part document, thus reducing by 80% the amount of paper used per year. Paper from well-managed forests is used, forests which have three trees replanted for every one felled.

The Post Office Community Involvement Programme has given major financial support to the Groundwork Trust's 'Brightsite' which seeks to improve the built environment in marginal areas. The Post Office staff secondment programme has provided skilled professional support to the National Trust and the British Trust for Conservation. The Post Office was also a founding corporate partner of 'Forum for the Future', a new charity set up by leading environmentalists.

All this information heartened me greatly. I had always been aware that I was part, even though a very small part, of an organisation which had always considered itself to be a service. This meant that its primary objective was a commitment to its users. Now I could more fully appreciate the extent of this commitment. I could appreciate even more fully its involvement in the over-riding consideration of reducing harm to the environment.

Its support of the arts I had always admired. So often one sees the words 'Post Office' in the list of sponsors for festivals, such as the Edinburgh Book Festival, when well-known writers are engaged to talk about their work. Books, too, have been supported, and the Post Office film unit has produced valued documentaries. In the children's Letter-writing Competition this year, on the theme 'Applying for my dream job', a record 500,000 young people, of whom 34,000 were from Scotland, responded. As one newspaper report said 'Despite hi-tech advances in communications, it appears that the art of letter-writing is alive and well.'

Artists have been encouraged to submit designs for new issues of pictorial stamps and over the years a collection of work of real merit has appeared. Posters, too, have been designed by artists of distinction. In these many, largely unsung, ways the Post Office has contributed to the cultural well-being of the country.

I am glad to have been involved with it, as part of a family concern, for close on forty years. And it's good to know that there are family members in the wings who have been part of the scene, too—a daughter who first stepped into the breach when the postmaster and his wife were temporarily laid low, to deliver the Christmas mails, and a grandaughter, now also a student, who date-stamped her own hands as a five-year-old and is now adept at date-stamping forms and dealing happily with customers as a holiday relief. That's how it goes in rural post offices.

It's really quite a unique position, that of a country postmaster. New types of job are being created now, in our age of telecommunication, but this one goes back for close on three hundred years, to the days of the Post-boys, the runners, then the mail coaches, now the steamer, the train, the plane. In all these times there was a Receiver and a Distributer of mail, a man at the centre, who saw, as we do today, beyond the paper-work, the customers, the human beings and their need to communicate. There's a good feeling of solidarity being part of a long tradition of service. The outcry is loud when a small office in a remote area is threatened with closure. That's surely proof, if one were needed, that the service is greatly valued.

Sources of Information

Jean Farrugia and Tony Gammons, *Carrying British Mails* (1980), from which the pictures on pp. 66, 79, 110, 113 and 124 are taken.

Dimitry Kandaouroff, *Collecting Postal History*

Dr James Mackay, *Islands Postal History* and other publications

Information Sheets from Post Office Archives, Freeling House, London

The Post Office, Scottish Post Office Board

Penrose Hay, *Post Office Recollections, Inverness 1885*

C.W. Hill, *Scotland in Stamps*

A.R.B. Haldane, *Three Centuries of Scottish Posts*